Letting Go
of the Past

*How to Overcome Overthinking,
Anxiety and Find Forgiveness*

BY J. J. NICOLLS

© Copyright 2024 - All rights reserved.

The content contained within this book may not be reproduced, duplicated or transmitted without direct written permission from the author or the publisher.

Under no circumstances will any blame or legal responsibility be held against the publisher, or author, for any damages, reparation, or monetary loss due to the information contained within this book, either directly or indirectly.

Legal Notice:

This book is copyright protected. It is only for personal use. You cannot amend, distribute, sell, use, quote or paraphrase any part, or the content within this book, without the consent of the author or publisher.

Disclaimer Notice:

Please note the information contained within this document is for educational and entertainment purposes only. All effort has been executed to present accurate, up to date, reliable, complete information. No warranties of any kind are declared or implied. Readers acknowledge that the author is not engaged in the rendering of legal, financial, medical or professional advice. The content within this book has been derived from various sources. Please consult a licensed professional before attempting any techniques outlined in this book.

By reading this document, the reader agrees that under no circumstances is the author responsible for any losses, direct or indirect, that are incurred as a result of the use of the information contained within this document, including, but not limited to, errors, omissions, or inaccuracies.

Dedication

To Lynn,

This book is dedicated to my sister. Your resilience through life's challenges is a testament to the strength within you. Your life's journey is characterized by poise and dignity, serving as a beacon for mine. May these pages reflect the beauty and courage you bring to every chapter of your life.

With deepest respect and love,

Your Baby Sister

Contents

Introduction 1

Chapter 1: The Paradox of Forgiveness: A Multifaceted Exploration 3

    Defining Forgiveness 4
    The Power of Letting 4
    Types of Forgiveness 5
    Why Forgiveness is Difficult 6

Chapter 2: The Neuroscience of Overthinking and Forgiveness: How Overthinking Can Hinder Forgiveness 9

    Overthinking and Its Impact on Healing: 10
    Neuroscience Behind Overthinking and Forgiveness Process 11

Chapter 3: The Brain on Forgiveness: Understanding the Neural Pathways 15

    Impact of Forgiveness on the Brain 16
    Neurological Functions Linked to Holding Grudges 17
    Role of Empathy in Forgiveness Pathways 18
    Neuroplasticity and the Practice of Forgiveness 19
    The Concert in Our Mind 20

Chapter 4: The Chemical Cocktail of Grudges: The Neurological Impacts of Resentment 23

    The Neurochemical Storm 24
    The Hormonal Havoc 25
    The Inflammatory Inferno 27
    The Gender Divide 27
    Breaking Free from the Grip of Grudges 28

Chapter 5: Rewire Your Brain for Forgiveness 29

    Muscle Memory 30
    The Science of Forgiveness Through Journaling 34
    Assignment 35

Chapter 6: Acknowledging and Understanding Your Emotions 39

    Unresolved Grief and Its Effect on Forgiveness 40
    Betrayal and Trust Issues in Relationships 40
    Childhood Trauma and Its Lasting Impact 41
    Emotional Abuse and Self-worth Struggles 42
    Complex Issues of Guilt, Shame, and Forgiveness 42
    The Role of Forgiveness: Letting Go and Healing 46
    Unraveling Guilt and Shame 47
    Two Powerful Activities 51
    Research that Self-Forgiveness Changes in Brain Activity .. 53

Chapter 7: Unearthing the Source: Identifying the Root
of Your Emotional Pain 55

    Identifying The Root Cause of Your Pain 57
    Examining the Impact of Suppressed Emotions 59
    Exploring Strategies for Recognizing and
    Accepting Emotions 60
    Unearthing Suppressed Emotions 61
    Assessing The Role of Empathy in Forgiveness 62
    Cultivating Resilience Through Emotional Healing 63

Chapter 8: The Empathy Connection: Mirror Neurons
and Understanding Others 65

    Biological Basis of Mirror Neurons 65
    Case Study of Mirror Neurons and Empathy 67
    Role Of Mirror Neurons in Social Cognition 68

Chapter 9: Memory and Forgiveness: Rewriting Painful Memories 71

Healing Through Reframing Traumatic Experiences 72
Rewriting Painful Memories: The Power of Empathy 72
Therapeutic Techniques for Rewriting Traumatic Memories 73
Emily's Transformation Through Reframing Trauma 74
Assignment 75

Chapter 10: Forgiveness and Sleep: The Role of the Subconscious Mind 79

Importance of Sleep on Forgiveness 79
Unconscious Healing Through the Subconscious Mind 82
How Forgiveness Impacts Dream Content 83
Psychological Benefits of Integrating Forgiveness and Sleep 84

Chapter 11: Confronting the Pain Without Being Overwhelmed 85

Facing the Hurt 85
Balancing Act 86
Small Steps 86
Support Systems 87

Chapter 12: The Art of Self-forgiveness: Neurological Pathways to Inner Peace 91

Definition Of Self-Forgiveness and Its Benefits 91
Self-Forgiveness VS Seeking Forgiveness from Others 92
Importance of Taking Responsibility for One's Actions 93
Decoding Self-Reflection: Your Brain's Guide to Healing ... 94

Chapter 13: Navigating Your Forgiveness Roadmap 97

    The Stages of Forgiveness: A Roadmap 97
    Samantha's Path to Serenity 105
    Navigating Setbacks 106
    The Power of Acknowledgment 107
    Assignment on "If I'm Facing Pain... Tools for
    Finding Your Way" 107

**Chapter 14: Seeking Professional Help: When to
Consider Therapy** 111

    Recognizing the Need 111
    The Role of Therapy 112
    Traditional Types of Therapeutic Approaches 113
    Technology and Forgiveness 113
    Overcoming Stigma 114

**Chapter 15: Moving Forward after Forgiveness: Setting
Boundaries, Self-care, and Gratitude** 117

    Importance of Setting Healthy Boundaries 117
    Boundaries: Protecting Your Progress 118
    Benefits of Prioritizing Self-care and Compassion 120
    Practicing Gratitude and Maintaining Positivity Daily 122

Conclusion 123

Glossary 127

References 135

Image References 139

Introduction

Have you ever found yourself staring into the darkness at 3 AM, the silence around you so profound that the beating of your own heart seems deafening? In those still hours, the past has a way of unraveling itself, replaying old hurts, and those wounds you thought had healed long ago are throbbing anew, their sting as sharp and fresh as it was the moment it was inflicted. This book is about silencing those thoughts during those introspective hours. It beckons you to delve into the maze of your heart, to navigate the twisted pathways of memories long buried but never forgotten.

We explore the stubborn persistence of these wounds and the reasons they refuse to fade into the bland tapestry of forgotten yesterdays. We'll understand that these echoes of the past are not mere ghosts meant to haunt us but are instead crucial fragments of the story that are uniquely ours. Acknowledging these hurts is not an act of dwelling in the past but a brave stride toward liberation. So, if you want to fix your heart for a better future, you must look at your past, no matter how painful it may be.

In the following chapters, we will embark on a journey—a journey not of forgetting but of understanding, not of erasing but of accepting. About recognizing that the keys to the prison of your past are in your hands, and that unlocking those doors is the first, courageous step toward a future where yesterday's shadows no longer dim tomorrow's light. So with open hearts and minds, let us begin this journey of healing, understanding, and, ultimately, profound transformation.

*Note: The content presented in this publication is solely for **educational purposes** and should not be considered as a replacement for expert medical counsel, diagnosis, or care. The* *material is derived from the author's research and does not claim to be an exhaustive resource on mental health matters.*

In case of a mental health crisis or urgent situation, it is imperative to seek immediate assistance from a professional. It is always advisable to consult a competent healthcare professional for any inquiries related to your mental health or medical interventions.

CHAPTER 1

The Paradox of Forgiveness: A Multifaceted Exploration

"To forgive is to set a prisoner free and discover that the prisoner was you."

- Lewis B. Smedes

Are you tired of the relentless chatter in your mind? Do you feel trapped in a cycle of overthinking, anxiety, and unresolved emotions? Does the weight of past hurts and grudges hold you back from experiencing true joy and peace? If so, this book is for you. In "Letting Go: How to Overcome Overthinking, Anxiety, and Find Forgiveness," we will explore the intricate connections between our thoughts, emotions, and well-being. Through practical techniques, insightful stories, and proven strategies, you will discover how to break free from the chains of overthinking, manage anxiety, and cultivate the power of forgiveness. This book will equip you with the tools to reclaim your inner peace, nurture healthy relationships, and create a life that radiates joy, resilience, and compassion.

Forgiveness is a deeply ingrained concept in human history and spiritual traditions. It has gained significant attention in contemporary research due to its profound effects on individual well-being and interpersonal relationships. Despite being widely recognized as a virtue, forgiveness is still a complex and multifaceted phenomenon that is often misunderstood and comes with challenges. This chapter aims to comprehensively explore forgiveness by defining it, discussing its various forms, exploring its underlying mechanisms, highlighting its associated benefits, and addressing the obstacles that often hinder its realization.

Defining Forgiveness

Forgiveness is often challenging to define precisely due to its inherent subjectivity and diverse interpretations. It is a deeply personal decision that involves actively choosing to let go of resentment, anger, and the desire for revenge toward those who have wronged us. This deliberate act is not a sign of weakness or condoning the offense, but rather a decisive decision to release negative emotions and move forward. Forgiveness can be extended to oneself, others, or even situations beyond human control, such as illnesses or natural disasters.

The Power of Letting

Letting go is not about forgetting or erasing the past; it's about releasing its grip on your present and future. It's a conscious choice to unburden yourself from the weight of resentment, regret, and pain, allowing yourself to move forward with grace and resilience. Letting go is a transformative act of self-love and forgiveness towards yourself and others. It's about reclaiming your power, rewriting your story, and opening your heart to new possibilities. It's an invitation to embrace the present moment fully, to live authentically, and to experience the profound freedom that comes from releasing what no longer serves you.

Forgiveness is a liberating experience that removes a heavy burden from one's shoulders. Research shows that forgiveness can have profound positive effects on both mental and physical health. It can strengthen interpersonal relationships, fostering empathy, compassion, and reconciliation. The psychological mechanisms underlying these effects include:

- The release of negative emotions.
- The restoration of a sense of control.
- The promotion of positive social interactions.

Types of Forgiveness

Forgiveness can take many forms, and understanding the distinct types can help one navigate the complex emotions involved in the process.

- Decisional forgiveness: Choosing to forgive in your mind.
- Emotional forgiveness: A genuine change in how you feel about the person who has hurt you.
- Silent forgiveness: Forgiving internally but not saying it to the person.
- Hollow forgiveness: Saying you forgive but still feeling angry or resentful.

Knowing the different forms of forgiveness is important for several reasons.

- It helps you recognize where you are in your own forgiveness process. Have you decided to forgive and truly let go of the pain? Knowing this can help you move forward.
- It helps you choose the right approach. If someone hasn't apologized, silent forgiveness might be the best option. If you're struggling with anger, emotional forgiveness might be the goal to work toward.
- It helps you communicate with others. If you understand the nuances of forgiveness, you can better explain your situation to the person who hurt you or to others who are supporting you.

- It can improve your relationships. Forgiveness is often key to healing and rebuilding relationships, and understanding how it works can lead to healthier connections.

- It benefits your well-being. Holding onto anger and resentment can harm your mental and physical health. Forgiving, in whatever form, can be a step toward peace and happiness.

Understanding the different types of forgiveness empowers you to navigate the complex emotions and choices involved, leading to personal growth and stronger relationships.

Why Forgiveness is Difficult

Forgiveness is often thought of as a quick and straightforward process, but in reality, it can be a long and challenging journey marked with setbacks and resurgences of pain. It's important to understand that there is no fixed timeline for forgiveness. It's crucial to honor your pace and emotional needs during this process. The pressure to forgive prematurely, whether from within or outside, may lead to inauthenticity that does not address the underlying cause of pain. Therefore, it's essential to approach forgiveness with patience and compassion toward yourself and others.

Forgiveness is often recognized as an important value, but it can be a challenging task to carry out. The reasons for this difficulty are multifaceted and rooted in human psychology.

When someone who has wronged us does not show remorse or take responsibility for their actions, forgiving them may seem insurmountable. The absence of regret or accountability can leave us grappling with conflicting emotions as we struggle to come to terms with our sense of injustice. Without closure and validation, the process of seeking forgiveness can be incomplete and unfair.

Furthermore, the fear of vulnerability and the risk of being hurt again can function as significant barriers to forgiveness. Being taken advantage of or traumatized again can hold individuals back from taking the necessary steps toward forgiveness.

It's important to note that forgiving someone does not mean the offense is forgotten or the past is erased. It's about accepting the pain, letting go of resentment, and making a deliberate decision to move forward. Of course, the hurtful memories may remain, and triggers can quickly reopen the healing wounds. As a result, the process of forgiveness may feel like a never-ending battle, needing constant effort and resilience.

In this chapter, "The Paradox of Forgiveness: A Multifaceted Exploration," we embarked on a journey through the labyrinth of forgiveness. We've recognized forgiveness as a dynamic process encompassing a spectrum of psychological states, from resentment to reconciliation. As we transition to Chapter Two, "The Neuroscience of Overthinking and Forgiveness: How Overthinking Can Hinder Forgiveness," we shift our lens from the philosophical to the physiological. This pivot in focus allows us to delve into the cerebral mechanisms that govern our thoughts and emotions and understand how the neural pathways involved in overthinking can obstruct the path to forgiveness.

CHAPTER 2

The Neuroscience of Overthinking and Forgiveness: How Overthinking Can Hinder Forgiveness

"Overthinking, also best known as creating problems that are never there."

- DAVID SIKHOSANA

Overthinking, a relentless loop of thoughts and worries, can feel like a prison cell for the mind. It traps us in a cycle of anxiety, self-doubt, and fear, often preventing us from experiencing true peace and joy. But what if we could understand the intricate workings of the brain that fuel this overthinking machine? What if we could unravel the neural pathways that keep us stuck in patterns of resentment and grudges, hindering our ability to forgive? In this chapter, we will explore the neuroscience of overthinking and forgiveness, exploring how our thoughts and emotions shape our brains and, ultimately, our lives. By understanding the underlying mechanisms, we can discover powerful strategies to break free from the grip of overthinking, cultivate forgiveness, and reclaim our mental well-being.

To begin with, it's important to have a clear understanding of overthinking and how it can affect a person's life. Overthinking is a state of continuously thinking about past occurrences or future possibilities, which can make it difficult for an individual to forgive and move forward. Constantly dwelling on negative thoughts and scenarios can intensify feelings of anger, resentment, and bitterness toward others.

Research has shown that overthinking triggers specific parts of the brain linked to stress and anxiety. This makes it challenging for people to release negative emotions and forgive others. By understanding these neural processes, we can gain valuable insights into how overthinking can hinder forgiveness.

Overthinking and Its Impact on Healing:

Remember this: Overthinking is a relentless mental loop of worries and anxieties that only hinders healing. It causes people to focus on the negative aspects of a situation, often magnifying small details and distorting them. This skewed thinking pattern can lead to increased feelings of anxiety and overall dissatisfaction with life.

Overthinking isn't just a personal struggle; it can also strain your relationships with others. When you ruminate over a past event, you trap yourself in a cycle of blame and resentment. This makes it incredibly hard to move on and let go of the pain.

It keeps you trapped in a state of distress, preventing you from moving forward and finding closure. It amplifies feelings of guilt, anger, or sadness, making it difficult to forgive ourselves or others. Moreover, overthinking often involves ruminating on past events or potential future scenarios, robbing us of the present moment. This inability to be fully present prevents you from engaging in activities promoting healing and enjoying life's simple pleasures.

Breaking free from the clutches of overthinking is essential for fostering healing. It's not enough to simply understand the issue; we must actively work to overcome it. By cultivating mindfulness, practicing self-compassion, and seeking support from loved ones or professionals, we can quiet the inner critic, release negative emotions, and create space for healing to occur. Remember, healing is not a linear process, and setbacks are a natural part of the journey.

Neuroscience Behind Overthinking and Forgiveness Process

Overthinking and forgiveness are closely related processes that result from the interplay between various brain regions and neurotransmitters. Overthinking often triggers increased activity in the prefrontal cortex, which controls decision-making, problem-solving, and self-control. This heightened activity can lead individuals to repeatedly replay negative thoughts and scenarios in their minds. The neuroscience behind these processes is complex and involves several brain functions and chemicals.

Research has proven that overthinking leads to abnormalities in the amygdala, a structure in the brain resembling an almond and nestled deep in the temporal lobe, which manages processing emotions such as fear and anger. If someone overthinks a situation involving hurt or betrayal, the amygdala can become hyperactive, leading to anxiety and distress.

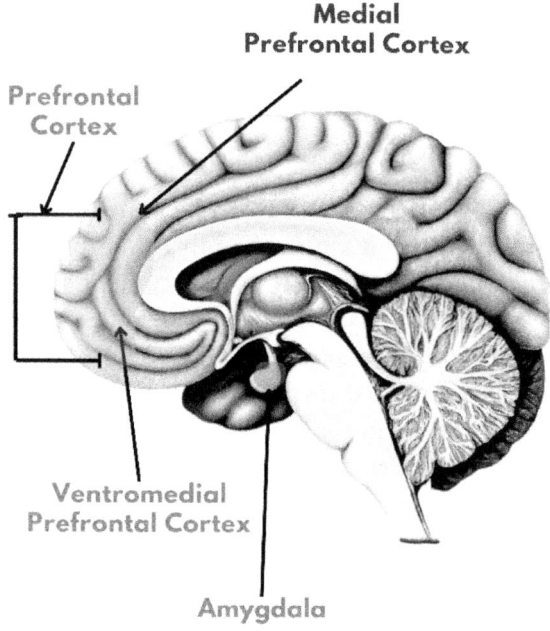

On the other hand, the forgiveness process engages distinct neural mechanisms connected with compassion and understanding. Research has shown that when individuals forgive someone who has wronged them, there is a noteworthy surge in activity within brain regions such as the anterior cingulate cortex (ACC) and insula—areas crucial for processing empathy and regulating emotions.

Forgiveness has also been linked to changes in specific neurotransmitters such as oxytocin and serotonin levels. Oxytocin, commonly known as the "love hormone", facilitates social bonding and trust. Forgiving others increases oxytocin levels, which promotes feelings of connection and closeness.

Serotonin is another neurotransmitter that takes part in controlling mood and emotional well-being. Forgiveness has been shown to boost serotonin levels in the brain, leading to a sense of peace and contentment.

Understanding the neuroscience behind overthinking and the forgiveness process can help individuals navigate challenging situations with more clarity and compassion. By recognizing how specific brain regions are activated during overthinking versus forgiveness, individuals can develop strategies to overcome rumination and cultivate forgiveness toward themselves and others for improved mental health

CHAPTER 3

The Brain on Forgiveness: Understanding the Neural Pathways

"Forgiveness is a gift you give yourself."
TONY ROBBINS

In the vast landscape of your brain, intricate neural pathways shape your thoughts, emotions, and actions. Forgiveness isn't just a simple act; it triggers a symphony of activity, profoundly rewiring our brains. In this chapter, we will explore the brain's response to forgiveness, delving into the neural mechanisms that underlie this transformative process. From releasing feel-good chemicals like dopamine and oxytocin to calming the amygdala, the brain's fear center, we will uncover the remarkable ways in which forgiveness heals, restores, and empowers us. Get ready to be amazed as we unravel the intricate dance of neurons that orchestrate the power of forgiveness.

The human brain is a wonder of complexity that holds the key to unlocking the power of forgiveness. Through the study of neural responses to forgiveness, we can understand how our minds process emotions and make decisions related to letting go of resentment.

Harboring grudges creates detrimental neurological patterns, which can be broken and remedied through the development of strategies to free ourselves from the cycle of resentment. Empathy, a powerful force, plays a crucial role in the journey toward forgiveness. By activating neural pathways associated with compassion and understanding, empathy paves the way for reconciliation and personal growth.

The concept of brain plasticity offers a beacon of hope, suggesting that forgiveness is not a fixed trait but a skill that can be cultivated. With practice and understanding, we can rewire our brains to embrace forgiveness, leading to lasting positive changes that improve our lives and build stronger relationships.

Impact of Forgiveness on the Brain

Recent research has shown that the parts of the brain responsible for empathy and perspective-taking are activated when we forgive. Forgiveness is mostly influenced by the anterior cingulate cortex, an area that is engaged in conflict management and emotion regulation. According to functional magnetic resonance imaging (fMRI) analyses, the ACC is more active when individuals are displaying forgiveness as opposed to times of non-forgiveness. People who are more inclined to forgive others also tend to be more engaged in processes associated with empathy, namely in trying to comprehend another person's view.

Studies have also shown that forgiveness might affect the body's physiological reactions. For example, research in heart rate variability (HRV), which measures the efficiency of the autonomic nerve system, has revealed that those more tolerant of others tend to have higher HRV levels than those less forgiving. According to these results, forgiving someone may help them become more adaptable and resilient by controlling their stress-related autonomic responses.

Forgiveness affects many different parts of the brain that work together to control emotions, show understanding, and understand other points of view. The fact that forgiveness changes how your autonomic nervous system works is another sign of how it might affect your general health.

Research on neuroplasticity has shown that long-term practices like forgiveness can lead to significant changes in the brain, particularly in areas involved in emotional processing. A compelling case study supporting this comes from the Picower Institute for Learning and Memory at MIT, where scientists discovered a fundamental rule of brain plasticity. They found that when one synapse strengthens, neighboring synapses weaken, which is a crucial aspect of how the brain keeps balance amidst new learning and experiences. This principle could extend to the practice of forgiveness, suggesting that as individuals engage in forgiveness, they may strengthen neural pathways associated with positive emotions and empathy, a direct and tangible effect of forgiveness on brain function. This adaptive capability of the brain underscores the potential for transformative psychological change through sustained mental practices like forgiveness.

Neurological Functions Linked to Holding Grudges

Researchers have been captivated by the intricate nature of grudge-holding in recent years. Unraveling the connections between neurotransmitters is a key step in understanding this complex emotional response. The amygdala is a focal point of this study. Studies have shown that it is more active during episodes of anger, suggesting its potential role in the persistence of negative emotions associated with long-held grudges.

Grudge-holding is not a simple emotional response, but a complex process that involves the prefrontal cortex, a region at the front of the brain. This area is responsible for our decision-making, impulse control, and social behavior. When this region is compromised, as seen in people who struggle to forgive, it becomes harder to let go of anger. Functional magnetic resonance imaging (fMRI) has revealed that those who find forgiveness challenging show less activity in the prefrontal cortex, making it difficult to manage their anger and empathize with those who have wronged them.

Neuroscientists have also found changes in the brain's connections associated with holding grudges. The default mode network (DMN) is linked to rumination, which angry people often engage in. Those who hold grudges have more significant connections in the DMN than those who are more forgiving, and the increased connection may make it easier for them to think negatively about past problems.

Recent research has also shed light on the crucial role of neurotransmitters in the brain processes related to forgiveness. Individuals who find it hard to release grudges often have lower levels of serotonin, a mood-regulating neurotransmitter. This deficiency in serotonin has been linked to increased aggression and decreased empathy, suggesting a direct link between neurotransmitter levels and the ability to forgive.

Meanwhile, oxytocin, known as the 'love hormone,' has been found to help forgiveness and promote kindness toward others. Studies have proven that administering oxytocin boosts trust and reduces feelings of betrayal, fostering a more accepting attitude.

Understanding the neurological basis of holding grudges offers valuable insights into the complex relationship between emotions, cognition, and brain function. By identifying the areas in the brain involved in this phenomenon, researchers are working on developing interventions that promote forgiveness and reduce the burden of unresolved resentment.

Role of Empathy in Forgiveness Pathways

The process of forgiveness can indeed be intricate and challenging, especially when someone has hurt us. However, empathy can play a crucial role in this process. This incredible ability allows us to understand and relate to the experiences and emotions of those who have caused us pain, ultimately leading us toward forgiveness.

Our brain's anterior cingulate cortex (ACC) oversees our emotions and resolves conflicts. When we feel genuine sympathy toward someone, this part of our brain becomes highly active. On the other hand, mirror neurons are also important for empathy as they enable us to understand how others feel by reflecting their actions and emotions in our brains. In essence, these neurons allow us to perceive the feelings and intentions of others.

Other psychological factors, such as perspective-taking and affective arousal, also amplify empathy and forgiveness. Perspective-taking helps us understand why someone might have acted wrongfully, while affective arousal fosters compassion rather than hostility, breaking down barriers between victims and offenders by instilling a sense of shared humanity.

In essence, people who are empathetic or good at understanding the emotions of others are more likely to act kindly toward others and less likely to be aggressive. This kindness toward others can help us forgive them, empathize with them, and build better relationships. So empathy is crucial for us to be more forgiving and help us heal emotional wounds.

Neuroplasticity and the Practice of Forgiveness

Forgiveness is a great act that can positively affect our physical and mental health. But have you ever wondered how our brain enables us to forgive someone who has hurt us? Our brain has an amazing capability called neural plasticity, which allows us to change how we think and feel about things.

When we are betrayed or hurt, the amygdala triggers negative emotions like anger and fear. But by practicing forgiveness repeatedly, our brain's neural plasticity comes into play. Over time, it can make the amygdala less active during situations related to forgiveness. This helps us let go of negative emotions and move forward.

As stated earlier, the prefrontal cortex helps us control and regulate our emotions, allowing us to make better decisions. When we practice forgiveness, we can improve the connections between the prefrontal cortex and the amygdala, which enables us to better control our emotional responses.

Moreover, practicing forgiveness can also affect other parts of our brain involved in empathy and understanding other people's perspectives. This helps us to see things from a broader perspective and increases our empathy and compassion toward others.

The Concert in Our Mind

Picture the human brain as an orchestra, with each neuron a musician, each synapse a note, and the act of forgiveness a complex, beautiful symphony. This marvel of nature, the brain, has long intrigued scientists and poets alike. Now, we're tuning our instruments and diving into a memorable melody: the neurological underpinnings of forgiveness. This essay is like a musical score, exploring the harmonies and rhythms of forgiveness as it resonates through the corridors of our minds, reshaping our thoughts and healing our hearts.

When we talk about forgiveness, we're not just discussing an emotional wave that washes over us. It's a whole symphony performed in the concert hall of our brains. Let's imagine walking through this hall, observing how each section of the orchestra plays its part in the forgiveness symphony.

First, we see the string section, the neural response to forgiveness. Here, the violins and cellos are regions of the brain, like the prefrontal cortex and the amygdala. They play a delicate balance, sometimes a tense melody of resentment, other times a soothing harmony of understanding and peace. Neuroimaging studies are like our concert maestros, revealing how these brain regions light up or quiet down during acts of forgiveness, creating a dynamic, ever-changing musical piece.

Next, we find the wind section, embodying the impact of forgiveness on brain health. Each flute and clarinet, each oboe and bassoon, plays notes that ripple through our neural pathways, bringing with them a breeze of benefits for our mental and physical well-being. These instruments sing of reduced stress, of harmonious neurotransmitter flows, and of the gentle aging of our cells, all orchestrated by the forgiving mind.

In a shadowed corner of our concert hall, the percussion section hints at the neurological correlation of holding grudges. The deep timpani and sharp snare drums echo the amygdala's throbbing pulse and the prefrontal cortex's tense grip. They beat a rhythm of rumination, a pattern hard to break but not impossible. Each drumroll reminds us of the challenge and the potential to transform this rhythm into a more harmonious tune.

The harp, with its gentle strings, personifies the role of empathy in forgiveness pathways. Each pluck resonates with understanding, each chord strums the strings of our mirror neurons. This part of the symphony invites us to step into another's shoes, to feel the vibrations of their experiences as if they were our own. It's a melody that softens hearts and opens doors to reconciliation.

Finally, the grand finale: neural plasticity and the practice of forgiveness. This is where the entire orchestra comes together, where the power of neuroplasticity allows the music to evolve and grow. Like a composer crafting a masterpiece, our brain rewires and adapts, turning dissonant chords into harmonious rhythms. This is the promise of forgiveness—a continuous, dynamic symphony that nurtures our ability to heal, connect, and thrive.

So here we are, in the grand concert hall of the brain, witnessing the symphony of forgiveness. It's a performance that speaks to the depth of our humanity, a melody that resonates with the potential for growth and change. As we explore this symphony, note by note, we not only deepen our understanding of the brain's pathways but also celebrate the profound impact of forgiveness on our lives and our societies.

Welcome to the symphony of forgiveness. May its music inspire and heal you.

As we turn the page from exploring the healing landscapes of forgiveness within the intricate neural pathways of the human brain, our journey brings us to a starkly contrasting terrain. This chapter was a serene stroll through the harmonious groves of empathy and understanding; the next will navigate the thorny thickets of the mind and why we hold grudges.

CHAPTER 4

The Chemical Cocktail of Grudges: The Neurological Impacts of Resentment

*"Holding onto a grudge is like drinking poison
and expecting the other person to die."*

- Unknown

Resentment, a silent but potent poison, brews a complex mixture of emotions and chemicals within the brain. This toxic blend sets off a destructive cycle, eroding our well-being and impeding our ability to heal and connect. We will uncover how resentment hijacks our brains and wreaks havoc on our lives, from the surge of stress hormones that flood our bodies to the dampening of pleasure chemicals that rob us of joy.

Holding a grudge may give the impression of having control, but it's a misleading illusion. Resentment hands control to the offender, consuming our thoughts while they move on. Like a heavy burden, the weight of the grudge drags us down, severely hindering our ability to heal and grow.

Scientific research reveals that resentment leaves a tangible mark on our brains, affecting our emotional and physical health. It impacts everything from our relationships to our overall well-being. But there is a beacon of hope! We will uncover the path that guides us back to the light, showing how conscious effort and awareness can liberate us from grudges. The brain's incredible adaptability empowers us to learn to let go, heal, and move toward harmony. By understanding the workings of resentment, we can break free and reclaim our power to live more satisfying lives.

We will uncover the complex chemical reactions triggered by grudges and explore their far-reaching consequences for our minds and bodies. When we hold onto resentment, we give the offender and the offense power over our thoughts and emotions. Meanwhile, the offender may remain unaware and move on with their life while we are still trapped in a cycle of negativity. This grudge becomes a psychological burden that drags us down like stones in a backpack on a difficult climb.

The Neurochemical Storm

At the heart of the grudge's impact on the brain is a disruption in the delicate balance of neurotransmitters, the chemical messengers responsible for regulating our mood and emotions. Two key players in this intricate dance are serotonin and dopamine.

Serotonin, often called the "feel-good" neurotransmitter, plays a crucial role in regulating mood, sleep, appetite, and even our ability to learn and remember. Chronic stress, a hallmark of holding grudges, depletes serotonin levels, causing us to feel anxious and irritable. Low levels of serotonin can also make existing mental health problems worse or create new ones.

Dopamine, the neurotransmitter responsible for pleasure, motivation, and satisfaction, is also known as the "reward" neurotransmitter. Research shows that grudges can negatively impact our ability to feel joy and motivation. Holding on to negative thoughts can disrupt levels of dopamine. So it's essential to let go of grudges and focus on positive things to maintain a healthy and happy mindset.

Oxytocin, also known as the "love hormone," is critical for forming social connections. However, stress can negatively change its production, leading to reduced social bonding and increased feelings of loneliness.

The Hormonal Havoc

Grudges also wreak havoc on our hormonal balance, primarily through the chronic activation of the stress response system. Two major players in this system are cortisol and adrenaline.

The adrenal glands release cortisol in response to perceived threats or stressors. When we hold grudges, our bodies stay in a state of heightened alert, perceiving the unresolved conflict as a constant threat. This leads to chronically elevated cortisol levels, which have been linked to a wide range of health problems, including:

- **Weakened Immune System.** Cortisol suppresses the immune system, making us more susceptible to infections and illnesses.

- **Cardiovascular Disease.** High cortisol levels contribute to hypertension (high blood pressure), atherosclerosis (hardening of the arteries), and other cardiovascular conditions.

- **Metabolic Disorders.** Chronic stress can disrupt metabolism, increasing the risk of developing insulin resistance, type 2 diabetes, and obesity.

- **Digestive Issues.** Cortisol can interfere with digestion, leading to symptoms such as stomach pain, bloating, and constipation.

- **Sleep Disturbances.** Elevated cortisol levels can disrupt sleep patterns, making it difficult to fall and stay asleep.

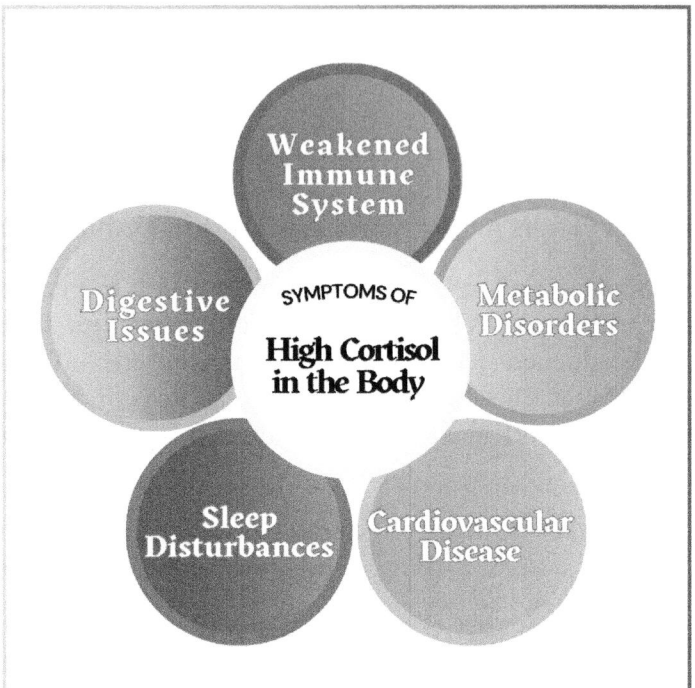

Adrenaline, also known as epinephrine, is another hormone involved in stress response. When we experience a perceived threat, adrenaline surges through our bodies, preparing us for fight or flight. While this can be beneficial in short bursts, the chronic activation of the adrenaline system due to grudges can lead to:

- **Anxiety and Panic Attacks.** Adrenaline fuels anxiety, making individuals more prone to panic attacks and other anxiety disorders.

- **Muscle Tension.** Adrenaline can cause muscles to tighten, leading to headaches, back pain, and other musculoskeletal problems.

- **Chronic Fatigue.** Stress and adrenaline release can eventually lead to exhaustion and fatigue.

The Inflammatory Inferno

Grudges not only disrupt our neurochemical and hormonal balance but also ignite an inflammatory response within our bodies. Inflammation is a natural part of the immune system response, but when it becomes chronic, it can have devastating consequences for our health.

Holding grudges triggers the release of pro-inflammatory cytokines—small proteins that function as signaling molecules within the immune system. Chronic inflammation has been linked to numerous health conditions, including:

- **Heart Disease.** Inflammation plays a pivotal role in the development of atherosclerosis, the build-up of plaque in the arteries that can lead to heart attacks and strokes.

- **Autoimmune Disorders.** Chronic inflammation can contribute to the development of autoimmune diseases such as rheumatoid arthritis, lupus, and multiple sclerosis.

- **Cancer.** Research suggests that chronic inflammation can create an environment conducive to cancer growth and progression.

- **Neurodegenerative Diseases.** Inflammation has been implicated in the development of neurodegenerative diseases like Alzheimer's and Parkinson's disease.

The Gender Divide

Interestingly, research suggests that the impact from the stress of grudges may differ between men and women. Studies have found that men tend to experience increased testosterone levels. Testosterone is a hormone associated with aggression and dominance, and elevated levels may contribute to increased anger and impulsive behavior.

On the other hand, women may experience fluctuations in estrogen levels. Estrogen is a hormone involved in mood regulation, and imbalances can exacerbate feelings of sadness, anxiety, and depression.

Breaking Free from the Grip of Grudges

There is encouraging news: the brain's remarkable ability to change holds the promise of healing from the toxic effects of grudges. By actively choosing to forgive, individuals can start a process of neural rewiring, enabling them to break free from the cycle of resentment and embrace positive emotions. Neural rewiring and forgiveness can be achieved through various techniques outlined in later chapters.

In this chapter, we explored resentment and persistent anger. We learned there are reasons why letting go is so difficult, such as chemicals in your brain that make you cling to the past. Holding on to these grudges hinders your progress toward healing. Yet every venture through darkness leads to a beacon of light. Escaping the thickets of grudges unveils a fresh chapter, beckoning us into the soothing realms of forgiveness.

CHAPTER 5

Rewire Your Brain for Forgiveness

> *"You have brains in your head. You have feet in your shoes. You can steer yourself any direction you choose."*
>
> - Dr. Suess

Imagine your brain as a complex tapestry of interwoven threads, each representing a thought, emotion, or memory. Some threads are vibrant and joyful, while others are tangled and knotted with pain and resentment. Forgiveness is the needle that can unravel these knots, releasing their grip on your mind and heart. In this chapter, we will journey, exploring the power of neuroplasticity - the brain's remarkable ability to change and adapt - to rewire our neural pathways for forgiveness. We will delve into the science behind forgiveness, uncovering how it can heal old wounds, dissolve grudges, and cultivate greater compassion and understanding. Through practical exercises and powerful insights, you will learn how to reshape your brain's landscape, creating a fertile ground for forgiveness to flourish. Prepare for a a life-changing adventure that will empower you to break free from the chains of resentment and embrace a future filled with peace and renewed connection.

We now recognize that forgiveness is more than a mere act; it's a process that reshapes our thoughts and heals our hearts. We will confront the myths that shroud forgiveness in misconceptions and light the path to understanding its true essence and immense benefits.

Muscle Memory

Muscle memory is a fascinating phenomenon that allows us to perform certain tasks automatically without conscious effort. It is the result of repetitive practice and the strengthening of neural connections in our brains. One excellent example of muscle memory is tying your shoe. Another example can be found in the memorization of multiplication tables. Understanding how muscle memory works can help us appreciate its importance and apply it to other areas of our lives. It can be applied to various skills, such as playing an instrument, learning a new skill, and even forgiveness. By practicing consistently over time, we can develop muscle memory that allows us to perform these activities easily and precisely.

When we first learn to tie our shoes, it requires a great deal of concentration and effort. However, with repeated practice, the process becomes automatic. Our muscles remember the specific movements needed to create a secure knot, allowing us to tie our shoes effortlessly without even thinking about it.

Another example is when we memorize multiplication tables through repetition and practice, we develop muscle memory for these calculations. This enables us to quickly recall the correct answers without having to consciously think about each step involved in solving them.

Similar to how repeated physical actions create muscle memory in the body, repetitive thought patterns and emotional responses can create a type of "emotional muscle memory" in the brain. This can make it difficult to forgive, as the brain becomes habituated to feelings of resentment or anger. However, just as physical therapy can retrain muscles, intentional practices like mindfulness and compassion can help rewire the brain's emotional responses.

One compelling case study, conducted with meticulous scientific rigor, unequivocally demonstrates the profound impact of guided meditation and forgiveness exercises on brain function. This meticulously researched evidence unequivocally shows a substantial decrease in the activity of brain regions associated with anger and a significant increase in the activation of areas linked to empathy and compassion. These findings establish that forgiveness is not an innate trait but a skill that can be honed through disciplined practice, resulting in a tangible change in the brain's emotional processing circuitry. This conclusively supports the notion that forgiveness, like any learnable skill, can be systematically cultivated, progressively reshaping the brain's habitual emotional response patterns. Saampras Ganesan and colleagues conducted this groundbreaking study as part of a collaboration between the Department of Psychiatry at the Melbourne Neuropsychiatry Centre and the Meditation Research Program at Massachusetts General Hospital.

"Harnessing Habitual Forgiveness: Building Muscle Memory for Emotional Agility"

Forgiveness is not just a moral virtue; it's a complex emotional skill that can be sharpened over time. Just as musicians practice scales to perform without conscious thought, we can train our emotional reactions to default to forgiveness through repetition and intention.

The journey to habitual forgiveness begins with recognizing it as a choice and making a commitment to that choice. It's about establishing a regular mental workout routine where forgiveness exercises are performed. Over time, these exercises increase our capacity for forgiveness, just like lifting weights increases our physical strength.

Emotional agility is about navigating life's challenges with a mindful, values-driven approach. As we develop muscle memory for forgiveness, we enhance our emotional agility, becoming adept at managing our reactions and emotions, leading to better decision-making and problem-solving.

Developing a new habit requires a strategic approach that incorporates several key steps. The first step involves setting a clear and specific goal. By defining the desired outcome, individuals can better direct their efforts and focus on what needs to be accomplished. For instance, if one aims to incorporate making your bed into their daily routine, they will set their goal as "making the bed daily".

Once the objective is established, creating a plan of action is crucial. By doing so, individuals can increase their chances of success. In our first example, someone might start immediately upon arising to make the bed. By scheduling a specific time each day, you will start to develop a routine.

Another essential step in building a new habit is finding potential obstacles that may impede progress. It is vital to anticipate challenges beforehand and develop strategies to overcome them effectively. For instance, if time constraints are an issue when trying to establish a new habit of your making the bed, one could explore options such as setting your alarm two minutes earlier in the morning to incorporate enough time, or possibly laying out your clothes the night before to find a little extra time.

Furthermore, using positive reinforcement plays a fundamental role in forming habits. By rewarding oneself for completing each step toward the desired behavioral change, individuals can reinforce positive associations with the new habit and motivate themselves to continue progressing. These rewards can take various forms depending on personal preferences. For example, treating yourself to that special latte in the morning on your way to work.

Chapter 5

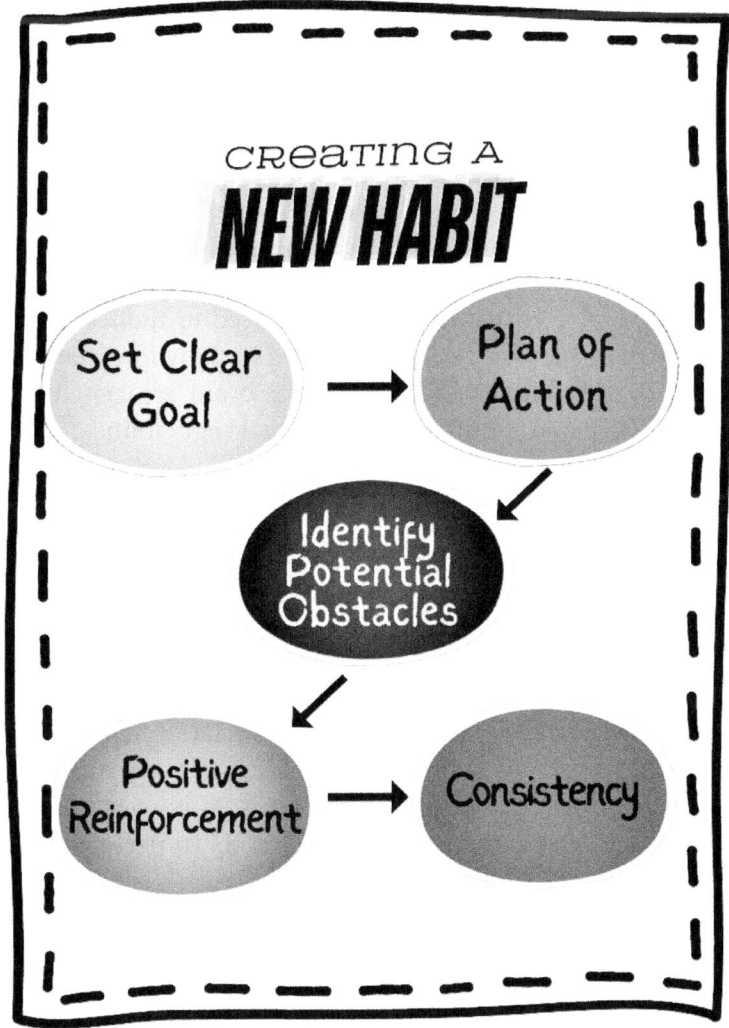

Lastly, consistency is key. Repetition helps solidify behaviors until they become automatic responses ingrained within one's daily life. Therefore, committing to practicing the desired behavior consistently over an extended period fosters its integration into everyday routines.

The Science of Forgiveness Through Journaling

As we already discussed, forgiveness is a complex psychological process that affects the mind and the body. Thus, we need to train the brain on how to forgive. Neuroplasticity (the brain's ability to reorganize itself by forming new neural connections) plays a pivotal role in the process. We need to induce muscle memory to foster forgiveness. Engaging in daily forgiveness of small things will lead to changes in the brain associated with empathy, decision-making, and emotional regulation.

Muscle memory is formed through myelination, where neural pathways are strengthened by wrapping them in a fatty substance called myelin. The more we repeat a task or action, the more myelin is produced around those neural connections, making them faster and more efficient.

Understanding muscle memory has practical applications beyond tying shoes or memorizing multiplication tables. It can be applied to various skills, such as playing an instrument or learning a new skill. By practicing consistently over time, we can develop muscle memory that allows us to perform these activities easily and precisely.

The following suggestions will allow the art of forgiveness to become a habit and, through repetition, form muscle memory on how to forgive:

- **Setting a Goal:** Recognize 10 small acts that you will forgive a day.

- **Creating a Detailed Plan:** Journal these 10 small acts as they happen.

- **Anticipating Obstacles:** Consider typing the journal entry on a smartphone or tablet computer if you forgot to bring your journal. You can also find a pen and scrap paper to write it down.

- **Utilize Positive Reinforcement:** Treat yourself to a desert or a night out every time you forgive something or someone.

- **Maintain Consistency:** Do it daily for at least 21 days.

This simple activity will also allow the art of forgiveness to become a habit and, through repetition, to form muscle memory on how to forgive and train the brain. This chapter delved into the psychological and physiological sides of forgiveness. Engaging in productive practices can lead to changes in the brain associated with empathy, decision-making, and emotional regulation, illustrating the brain's adaptability to foster forgiveness. The key is to start small. Nobody runs a marathon on their first day; they start by walking or running for a short distance and increase it as they become better trained.

Assignment

Get a notebook or journal. It does not need to be anything fancy but small enough that it is easy to carry around.

Find ten simple, non-threatening actions that happen daily and mindfully forgive them. For example, when setting the table, you or someone else forgot to put the salt and pepper out. When you go down to enjoy your delicious meal, you realize no seasoning is available.

Mindfully forgive yourself or someone for forgetting about it. This will be more difficult than you think because you are trained to fix the problem by getting up and getting it yourself or barking a comment. But the act, although it may be annoying, is harmless. Another example is that you might forget to take the clothes out of the washer and place them into the dryer, giving them a musty smell. You now must rewash it. Or someone may be three minutes late picking you up.

Regardless of the severity, the idea is to find 10 occurrences daily that you mindfully forgive for at least 21 days.

Why 21 days? According to a study in 2009 published in the European Journal of Social Psychology, it takes anywhere from 18 to 254 days for a person to form a new habit. However, these figures can vary greatly depending on the complexity of the habit and the individual's circumstances. It's important to remember that forming a new habit is a process that requires patience and consistency.

So yes, you may have to do it longer. In the beginning, make sure your journal entries are incredibly detailed. As time passes, you can shorten them, but continue to write them down and repeat forgiveness in your mind.

Forgiveness Entry:

> *I chose to forgive my son, John, for forgetting the salt and pepper when setting the table. I understand that he, like everyone else, can make mistakes and may not always do things perfectly. I acknowledge my frustration, but I choose not to hold on to this negativity. Instead, I release it and replace it with understanding and compassion. I forgive John.*

> Then follow it with a **Gratitude Entry:**

> *I am grateful for the support of my son, who relieved me of the duty of placing the napkins, plates, silverware, and other condiments on the table. His kind words and*

understanding helped me navigate through this situation. I am also grateful for the personal strength I discovered in myself today. It reminded me that I have the ability to control my reactions and emotions. Lastly, I am grateful for the lesson this situation taught me about empathy and forgiveness.

To forgive is to let go of anger and bitterness against a person or group that harmed you, regardless of whether they deserve your forgiveness or not. The healing process goes beyond accepting apologies; it needs a deep emotional and cognitive shift on the inside.

We have started our life-altering quest, following the winding roads of forgiveness as a means of healing, and letting go. Our journaling will allow us to rewire our brains, so forgiveness becomes second nature.

Yet the journey to forgiveness is multilayered, often requiring us to confront and understand the full spectrum of our emotions. As we close this chapter, we stand at the threshold of a deeper exploration, ready to delve into the very heart of our emotional world.

Continue with the process of journaling for at least 21 days. It is designed to be done simultaneously with the chapters that follow. However, before moving on to the next chapter, jot down an entry in your journal or on a scrap of paper of a small act to which you can offer forgiveness.

CHAPTER 6

Acknowledging and Understanding Your Emotions

"The emotion that can break your heart is sometimes the very one that heals it..."

- NICHOLAS SPARKS

We will visit the sacred space of your own emotions in this chapter. Here, we start to work on that one issue that made you decide to pick up this book in the first place. We will recognize that forgiveness and forgiving someone is not a one-and-done deal but rather an ongoing process that requires us to tune into and confirm our emotions.

This chapter is an invitation to an inward journey, where acknowledging and accepting your emotions becomes the cornerstone of genuine healing and forgiveness. We will explore how recognizing our emotional landscape is not a sign of weakness but a brave step toward self-awareness and growth.

Together, we will learn how to navigate through the complexities of our feelings, understanding that each emotion carries a message that, when listened to, can guide us toward deeper insight and clarity. We will discover tools and techniques to gently uncover and address the layers of hurt, anger, disappointment, or betrayal that may be hindering your path to forgiveness.

Unresolved Grief and Its Effect on Forgiveness

Unresolved grief can leave deep emotional scars, making it difficult to forgive those who have hurt us. When we experience a significant loss or betrayal, it is imperative to confront and work through these feelings. Otherwise, this grief can manifest as deep sadness, anger, or resentment, which can weigh heavily on our minds and hearts, making it challenging to find peace or forgive others. This is why we experience an intense emotional outburst when triggered by the reminder, however slight, of a painful past event.

Moreover, grief can fuel guilt and self-blame. We may wonder what we could have done differently to avoid the pain we are feeling, while self-doubt can worsen our scars, making it harder to forgive ourselves for any mistakes we believe we may have contributed to the event.

You may feel trapped in an endless cycle, which can make it difficult to heal your deep-seated wounds and even more challenging to forgive those who caused you pain. However, when we confront the situation that led to our pain, we open the door to true healing and the potential to extend forgiveness to those who have hurt us. Our primary goal is to acquire a comprehensive understanding of this topic, guiding you through the complexities of forgiveness. This understanding will equip you with the tools for healing and personal growth.

Betrayal and Trust Issues in Relationships

Betrayal and the breaking of trust can cause severe damage to a relationship. It can be incredibly devastating when someone you trusted violated that trust, which can undermine the foundation of the bond between them and you. For instance, a partner cheating on you or a close friend spreading rumors about you. These wounds will run deep and leave long-lasting pain that can be challenging to overcome.

This heartache can bleed into other aspects of your life, fostering skepticism and making it difficult to trust again. The easy response is to build walls around your heart to shield yourself from future pain. However, true healing is a gradual process that requires finding the courage to gradually let trusted people in. It's a slow process but an important one, and you're not alone on this journey.

To truly address your pain, explore the roots of your trust issues. This might involve revisiting uncomfortable memories or confronting past traumas. This journey of self-discovery and acceptance is where true healing begins. Face your vulnerabilities, acknowledge your pain, and find the strength to release it. This process, though challenging, holds the potential for profound personal growth—a testament to your strength and resilience.

Childhood Trauma and Its Lasting Impact

Childhood trauma is a significant issue that can leave lasting scars, altering the course of a person's life. These experiences disrupt the delicate process of personality development in childhood. Neglect or abuse can create distorted self-perceptions and unhealthy coping mechanisms. The impact echoes into adulthood, blurring past and present, damaging relationships, and making forgiveness a formidable challenge.

It creates vulnerability, difficulty trusting others, and a tendency to misinterpret actions as threats. This makes forgiving others an incredibly challenging task when trust feels impossible. The impact is also not limited to emotional scars. Research links childhood trauma to an increased risk of chronic diseases, demonstrating the connection between mental and physical health.

Furthermore, childhood trauma can have multi-generational consequences. Studies suggest trauma can leave marks on DNA, impacting future generations. This realization amplifies the weight of forgiveness, as the healing process holds implications for your loved ones. Its complex and far-reaching consequences make forgiveness a complicated feat. But understanding its profound impact is crucial in the journey toward healing and finding the strength to forgive oneself and others.

Emotional Abuse and Self-worth Struggles

If you are a survivor of emotional abuse, it's important to recognize that the tactics of relentless criticism, manipulation, and isolation used by the abuser were not your fault. You are not to blame for what happened to you, and you deserve to reclaim your self-worth and self-confidence.

It's common for survivors of emotional abuse to feel a desperate need for validation, which can mask a profound lack of self-confidence. However, by recognizing this and working toward rebuilding your self-worth, you can start to regain a positive self-image and a sense of your inherent value.

Setting healthy boundaries can be challenging after experiencing emotional abuse, but it's an important step toward healing. You may need to work with a therapist or a trusted friend to regain trust in others and learn how to set boundaries that protect your emotional well-being.

Remember, healing from emotional abuse is a journey, and it's important to be patient and kind to yourself along the way. Only then can you embark on a path toward forgiving yourself and others and rediscovering your inherent value.

Complex Issues of Guilt, Shame, and Forgiveness

Emotional wounds, like physical injuries, require time and proper care to heal. However, unlike physical injuries, emotional wounds can be more complicated as they are connected to our identity and past experiences. Unraveling emotions like guilt, shame, and forgiveness can be tricky, as they are often painful. But while they co-exist, they aren't interchangeable. Understanding their differences is crucial for navigating the complex web they create within us.

The Sting of Guilt: Taking Responsibility for Actions

Guilt arises from a specific action or inaction believed to be wrong. It's a self-directed emotion, a gnawing feeling that tells us we've violated our moral code or caused others harm. It motivates us to make amends, apologize, or rectify the situation.

For example, if you accidentally spill coffee on a colleague's important documents, guilt prompts you to apologize and offer to replace them. It's a constructive emotion, driving us toward amendment and making it less likely we'll repeat the mistake.

The Crushing Weight of Shame: Feeling Flawed at the Core

Shame, on the other hand, digs deeper. It is a broader, often more debilitating emotion that attacks our sense of self-worth. It whispers that we are fundamentally bad or unlovable due to our actions or simply because of who we are.

Imagine being bullied for your appearance. Shame might make you feel inadequate like you don't deserve to belong. It's a destructive emotion, isolating us and hindering our ability to move forward.

The Blurring Lines: When Guilt and Shame Intertwine

The lines between guilt and shame can become blurry. Sometimes, guilt can transform into shame if we dwell on the transgression excessively. The "I messed up" can morph into "I'm a terrible person."

Further complicating the picture, shame can also masquerade as guilt, leading us to take an excessive amount of blame or self-punish for things beyond our control. This can happen in abusive situations, where a victim internalizes the abuser's blame and feels inherently bad.

Guilt or Shame?

This questionnaire is intended to help you identify whether you are experiencing guilt, shame, or a combination of both. Please read each statement and indicate how often you feel this way by circling the appropriate number.

Key:

1. Never
2. Rarely
3. Sometimes
4. Often
5. Always

Section 1: Guilt

1. I feel remorseful after making a mistake.

    1   2   3   4   5

2. I think about ways I can make amends when I've hurt someone.

    1   2   3   4   5

3. I believe that I've done something bad.

    1   2   3   4   5

4. I want to apologize or correct a wrong I've done.

    1   2   3   4   5

5. My feelings of regret are specific to certain actions I've taken.

   1   2   3   4   5

Section 2: Shame

1. I feel like I am a bad person.

   1   2   3   4   5

2. I want to hide or disappear whenever I think about my ugly parts.

   1   2   3   4   5

3. I feel unworthy of love or belonging.

   1   2   3   4   5

4. I often criticize myself harshly.

   1   2   3   4   5

5. I think others view me negatively or as a failure.

   1   2   3   4   5

Section 3: Reflection

1. When I feel bad about something, it's usually because of something I've done, not because of who I am.

   1   2   3   4   5

2. I believe that my mistakes make me unworthy as a person.

                1   2   3   4   5

3. I feel like I can change my behavior and make better choices next time.

                1   2   3   4   5

4. I think that if people knew the real me, they wouldn't like what they see.

                1   2   3   4   5

5. I recognize that everyone makes mistakes and that doesn't make them bad people.

                1   2   3   4   5

Scoring:

- Guilt: If you scored higher in Section 1, you might be experiencing guilt.
- Shame: If you scored higher in Section 2, you might be experiencing shame.
- Both: If you have high scores in both sections, you may be experiencing a mix of guilt and shame.

The Role of Forgiveness: Letting Go and Healing

In this tangled web, forgiveness acts as a potential pathway to healing. It doesn't erase the wrongdoing or excuse the offender's actions. Instead, it allows us to let go of the negative emotions associated with the incident. Here's the key distinction:

- **Forgiving ourselves:** We can forgive ourselves for a mistake by acknowledging the guilt, making amends if possible, and learning from the experience. This allows us to release the self-flagellation of shame and move forward with self-compassion.

- **Forgiving others:** Forgiving someone doesn't mean condoning their actions. It's more about letting go of resentment and anger, allowing us to detach emotionally from the offense and find peace. In some cases, it might not only allow us to move on but also pave the way for reconciliation, a possibility that can bring hope and healing.

Ultimately, the power to unravel the tangled web lies within you. The first step is self-awareness. Recognizing the difference between guilt and shame can empower you to move toward a place of self-compassion. Acknowledging the need for forgiveness, whether of yourself or others, opens the door to healing and letting go.

Remember, forgiveness is not always easy, nor it is linear. There will be setbacks and moments of doubt. However, with self-awareness, support, and a commitment to personal growth, you can untangle the web and move toward a more peaceful and forgiving way of being.

Unraveling Guilt and Shame

Guilt and shame are emotions that we all experience at some point in our lives. It's important to understand that although they are similar, they differ in how our brains process them. When we feel guilty, our brain activates the part that helps us distinguish right from wrong, while shame triggers the part that makes us aware of ourselves and causes us to feel bad about ourselves.

It's important to note that guilt and shame can negatively affect us if we don't deal with them. If we always feel guilty, we might start criticizing ourselves more harshly, and if we feel ashamed, our self-esteem can suffer. But we don't have to let these emotions control us. We can take charge, start to forgive ourselves and heal.

One effective way is through mindfulness, which means paying attention to our thoughts and feelings without judging them. Another way is through therapy, where we talk to someone about our feelings and get help changing the way we think about ourselves.

By taking action and actively rewiring our brains with positive thoughts, we can overcome these negative emotions and create a happier, healthier life for ourselves. So let's take the first step towards healing and start making positive changes in our lives.

Chapter 6

SHAME vs GUILT

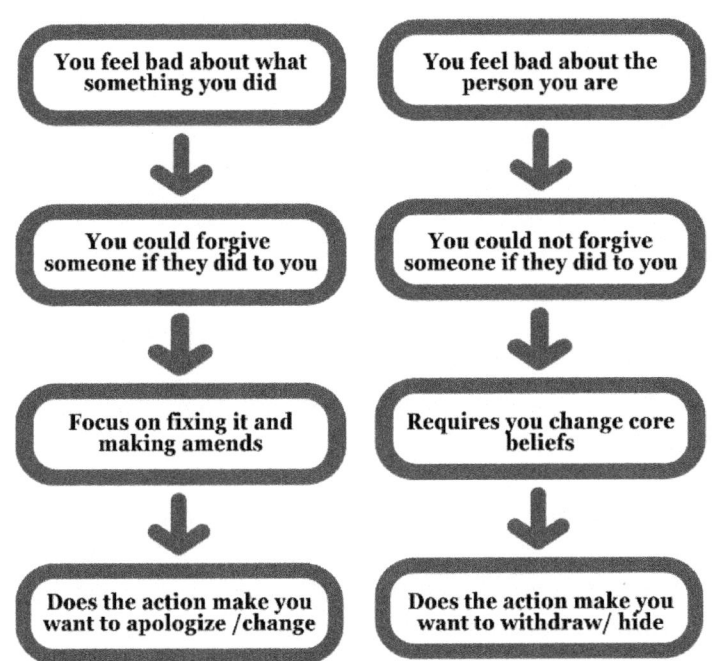

The Shame vs. Guilt Test

Purpose: To help you identify whether shame or guilt is the primary emotion you're experiencing in a given situation.

Instructions: Think of a Situation: Recall a recent event where you felt a strong negative emotion about your actions or words. Briefly describe it below:

_____

_____

_____

Answer the Questions: Circle the answer that best describes how you feel. There are no right or wrong answers; just be honest with yourself.

1. Do you feel bad about WHAT you did, or WHO you are?

    WHAT I DID　　　　　　　WHO I AM

2. Is your main focus on fixing something or feeling like a fundamentally flawed person?

    FIXING IT　　　　　　　FLAWED PERSON

3. Can you imagine someone else doing the same thing and feeling compassion for them?

    YES　　　　　　　NO

4. Does this experience make you want to apologize/change, or withdraw/hide?

    CHANGE　　　　　　　WITHDRAW

Scoring:

Mostly "WHAT I DID", "FIXING IT", "YES", and "CHANGE": Indicates you feel GUILT.

Mostly "WHO I AM", "FLAWED PERSON", "NO", and "WITHDRAW": Indicates you feel SHAME.

Interpreting Your Results:

Guilt: Focus on amends, changing behavior, seeking forgiveness if appropriate.

Shame: Requires challenging negative core beliefs, building self-compassion, potentially with a therapist's help.

Two Powerful Activities

The Compassionate Letter

Purpose: Aims to foster self-compassion by giving yourself the kindness and understanding you might extend to a loved one. It helps rewire neural pathways associated with self-criticism, promoting a more forgiving and supportive inner voice. This exercise creates a powerful foundation for self-forgiveness and self-worth.

Detailed steps:

1. Find a quiet, undisturbed space to minimize distractions.
2. Reflect on a specific past experience that triggers feelings of guilt or shame.
3. Visualize a younger version of yourself struggling with the aftermath of that experience.
4. Write a letter expressing the compassion, understanding, and forgiveness you wish you had received at that time.

5. Use kind and reassuring language, reminding your younger self that mistakes are part of learning and do not define them.

6. After writing, read the letter aloud slowly, truly allowing the words to resonate with your current self.

WHY IT'S POWERFUL: This exercise activates brain regions associated with empathy and self-love. It disrupts the cycle of self-criticism by replacing it with compassion, fostering a more positive internal dialogue.

Reframing Negative Beliefs

Purpose: Challenges the harmful thought patterns that perpetuate guilt and shame. By actively questioning these beliefs and replacing them with more balanced perspectives, you rewire your brain to respond more positively to challenges. This exercise fosters self-compassion, reduces emotional reactivity, and promotes self-forgiveness. Detailed steps:

- Identify a recurring negative belief about yourself related to past mistakes (e.g., "I'm a failure," "I'm unlovable").

- Challenge this belief by asking yourself:

- Is this 100% true in every situation? Can I think of exceptions?

- Would I say this to a friend? What would a compassionate person say to me instead?

- Find a more balanced and realistic alternative belief (e.g., "I made a mistake, I'm capable of learning," "I deserve love, even though I'm not perfect").

- Practice replacing the old belief with the new one whenever it arises in your mind. Consistency is essential for rewiring.

WHY IT'S POWERFUL: This exercise targets core beliefs that perpetuate self-blame and hinder forgiveness. With repetition, we shift from automatic negativity toward a more compassionate and realistic self-view.

Research that Self-Forgiveness Changes in Brain Activity

Self-forgiveness can actually rewire our brains. Research shows that forgiving ourselves has a tangible impact on brain activity by boosting activity in the prefrontal cortex and improving emotional regulation and decision-making. Moreover, self-forgiveness activates brain regions that promote empathy and compassion, both towards ourselves and others. All this has been scientifically proven and has been shown to lead to better relationships and overall well-being.

This is a powerful tool that can effectively rewire our brains by stimulating neuroplasticity. The impact of this process is immense - it allows us to heal old wounds, improve our emotional processing, and enhance our memory. The potential of forgiveness to transform us is immeasurable, as it not only enables an emotional shift but also optimizes how our brains function.

Imagine being free from the burdens of past mistakes, prioritizing personal growth and mental health. This is all possible with self-forgiveness. The brain's role is fascinating! Self-reflection can help us process guilt and shame, leading to a deeper understanding of our past choices. And the best part? Neuroplasticity provides a pathway for healing! By consciously choosing self-forgiveness, we can rewire these brain networks, empowering us to take control of our emotional well-being and foster greater resilience.

There's more! Scientific studies have uncovered the profound influence of self-forgiveness on our brains. It shows that it can change brain activity, enhancing our ability to regulate emotions, foster empathy, and healthily process memories. How amazing is that? This understanding equips us with the power to actively strive for a more forgiving mindset, enhancing our overall mental health.

Our journey through "The Art of Self-Forgiveness" has illuminated the power of rewiring our brains for inner peace. Now, let's delve into the fascinating world of mirror neurons. These brain cells, which echo the actions and emotions of those around us, can bring practical benefits to our lives. This understanding of ourselves and others equips us with tools to enhance our relationships, build stronger communities, and foster a more compassionate world. Could the secrets of mirror neurons be the key to unlocking our full potential for empathy? Our next chapter, " Seeking Professional Help: When to Consider Therapy," underscores the importance of professional guidance in our journey towards healing and forgiveness, providing a reassuring hand in our personal growth journey.

CHAPTER 7

Unearthing the Source: Identifying the Root of Your Emotional Pain

"Out of suffering have emerged the strongest souls; the most massive characters are seared with scars."

- KHALIL GIBRAN

We often experience emotional pain that is difficult to understand. This pain can be overwhelming, like being stuck in a murky swamp. However, just as a swamp can have a blocked stream, our emotional pain often comes from more profound, less obvious issues. The path to healing and freedom starts by identifying and dealing with the main cause of our emotional pain. This is our chance to remove the obstacles holding us back, allowing us to move forward with renewed courage and inspiration. Let's eagerly embark on this journey of self-discovery and take these steps:

- **Notice Your Emotional Triggers.** Pay attention to situations, people, or thoughts that consistently evoke negative emotions. Identifying these triggers can be like finding stepping stones leading toward the source of the pain. By recognizing and understanding these patterns, you can begin to develop strategies for managing your emotions and healing from past hurts

- Do you feel angry when criticized or sad after spending time with a particular friend?

- Are there certain places that bring up painful memories or feelings of unease?

- Do specific words or phrases trigger a strong emotional reaction within you?

- Are there certain times of day, year, or specific dates that consistently bring up difficult emotions?

- Do physical sensations, such as a racing heart or tightness in your chest, accompany these emotional triggers?

- Does your behavior change when you encounter these triggers? Do you withdraw, become defensive, or lash out?

- **Explore Past Experiences.** Sometimes, emotional pain is a lingering echo from past experiences. Have you experienced a significant loss, betrayal, or trauma? These events can leave scars that continue to impact your present emotions. Consider if past experiences might be influencing your reactions in current situations.

- **Uncovering Core Beliefs.** Often, emotional pain stems from underlying beliefs we hold about ourselves or the world. Do you believe that you're not good enough or that the world is a hostile place? These beliefs can color your feeling of events and trigger negative emotions. Journaling or talking to a therapist can help you uncover these hidden beliefs.

- **Putting It All Together.** Once you've identified your triggers, explored past experiences, and considered core beliefs, try to find the common thread. Does your fear of criticism stem from a childhood experience of being harshly judged? Does sadness after spending time with a particular friend connect to a belief that you're not worthy of a true connection? You can pinpoint the root cause of your emotional pain by connecting the dots.

Remember, this is a journey, not a destination. Patience and self-compassion are key. As you gain a deeper understanding of the source of your pain, you empower yourself to choose healthier responses and move toward emotional well-being.

Identifying The Root Cause of Your Pain

Understanding the underlying reasons for your emotional pain can lead to better coping strategies and personal growth. This questionnaire will guide you through a series of questions to help you uncover the root cause of your pain.

Instructions: Please read each question and reflect on your feelings and experiences. Take your time to write down your responses.

Section 1: Current Emotional State

1. Describe the emotional pain you are currently feeling.
2. On a scale of 1 to 10, how intense is this pain?

Section 2: Situational Analysis

1. Can you identify a recent event that triggered this pain?
2. What were the circumstances surrounding this event?

Section 3: Pattern Recognition

1. Have you felt this way before?
2. Are there common themes or situations that trigger this pain?

Section 4: Personal Beliefs and Values

1. What personal beliefs or values do you hold that might be related to this pain?

2. Do you feel these beliefs are being challenged or undermined?

Section 5: Behavioral Response

1. How do you typically react when you feel this pain?
2. Are there any coping mechanisms you resort to? Are they healthy or harmful?

Section 6: Physical Manifestations

1. Do you experience any physical symptoms associated with your emotional pain (e.g., headaches, stomachaches)?
2. How does your body feel overall during these emotional episodes?

Section 7: Impact on Daily Life

1. How does this pain affect your daily activities and relationships?
2. Are there things you avoid doing or people you avoid seeing because of this pain?

Section 8: Self-Reflection

1. What do you think is the deeper reason behind this pain?
2. Are there unresolved issues or past traumas that might be contributing to your current state?

Section 9: External Influences

1. Do external factors such as work stress, social pressures, or global events play a role in your pain?
2. How do these factors worsen or alleviate your pain?

Reflect on your answers and try to find patterns or recurring themes. Understanding the root cause of your pain is a significant step toward healing and finding peace. Consider discussing your findings with a trusted friend or a professional to gain further insights.

Examining the Impact of Suppressed Emotions

Suppressing emotions, often seen as a sign of strength or resilience, can have far-reaching consequences for mental and physical well-being. We have previously discussed its impact on our bodies, but it's worth repeating to emphasize its importance.

When we bury these feelings—anger, sadness, or fear—we don't actually make them disappear. Instead, they simmer beneath the surface, consuming energy, and they can manifest in unexpected ways. They can appear in the form of increased anxiety, irritability, difficulty in concentrating, and even physical symptoms like headaches and digestive issues. In essence, emotional suppression becomes a ticking time bomb, waiting to explode. It's important to be aware of these potential risks to our mental and physical well-being.

On a physiological level, suppressed emotions deregulate the stress response system. The body stays in a heightened state of alert, flooding with cortisol and adrenaline. Over time, this chronic stress weakens the immune system, increases the risk of cardiovascular diseases, and worsens existing health conditions. Mentally, the inability to process emotions can lead to a sense of emotional numbness, difficulty connecting with others, and a distorted self-perception.

Exploring Strategies for Recognizing and Accepting Emotions

Recognizing and accepting our emotions can be challenging, but it is crucial for our mental and emotional well-being. If you're struggling to process your feelings, there are several powerful strategies you can try.

Start by paying attention to your body's signals. Our emotions often manifest physically through tension headaches, stomachaches, or changes in sleep patterns. By noticing these physical sensations, we can trace them back to their emotional roots.

Journaling can also be a highly effective tool. Writing down your thoughts and feelings without judgment allows you to explore whatever appears on the page. This practice can help you identify patterns in your emotions and uncover those that have been suppressed.

Practices like meditation or yoga can also help you become more aware of your emotions. They encourage you to be fully present in the moment, allowing you to tune in to your inner experiences without judgment. By observing your thoughts and feelings with curiosity and compassion, you can identify and accept emotions hidden beneath the surface.

Remember, acknowledging and accepting your emotions is not about wallowing in negativity or dwelling on past hurts. It's about recognizing the full spectrum of human experience and permitting yourself to feel. By embracing our emotions, positive and negative, we cultivate a greater sense of self-awareness and develop healthier coping mechanisms for dealing with life's challenges.

If you struggle to identify and accept your emotions, seeking professional help can be incredibly beneficial. A therapist can provide guidance and support in exploring your emotional landscape and developing healthy strategies for processing complicated feelings. Seeking help is a sign of strength and is needed for healing and self-discovery.

Unearthing Suppressed Emotions

Step 1: Body Scan and Awareness (5 minutes)

1. Location & Posture: Write about the quiet, comfortable place you chose and your relaxed position.
2. Breathing: Note your experiences and sensations during the deep breathing exercise.
3. Body Scan Observations: Record any sensations in different body parts, starting from toes upwards. Mention areas of tension or discomfort.

Step 2: Emotional Check-In (5 minutes)

1. Current Emotional State: Describe your feelings at the moment without judgment or pressure.
2. Emotions Identified: List any emotions that arise. Example: "Tightness in chest," "Sadness in the stomach."

Step 3: Memory Exploration (10-15 minutes)

1. Triggering Event: Briefly describe the situation or event that evoked a strong emotional response.
2. Sensory Recall: Detail what you saw, heard, smelled, tasted, or felt in that situation.
3. Physical Reactions: Note any physical reactions to the memory.
4. Hidden Emotions: List the emotions you believe might be underlying in the memory.

Step 4: Creative Expression (10-15 minutes)

1. Creative Outlet Chosen: Specify the medium of creative expression you chose (journaling, drawing, etc.).
2. Expression of Emotions: Describe your experience and feelings during this creative expression.

Step 5: Reflection and Self-Compassion (5 minutes)

1. Emotional Insights: Share the emotions you uncovered and any surprises during the exercise.
2. Self-Compassion Reflection: Reflect on any discomfort and offer yourself compassion. Acknowledge your progress.

Assessing The Role of Empathy in Forgiveness

To truly forgive, we must first understand the deep connection between empathy and emotional healing. Emotions, especially those tied to painful experiences, leave lasting imprints that can hinder our ability to forgive. Understanding our feelings is a crucial aspect of personal growth and well-being. Empathy is the key to unlocking this understanding, allowing us to navigate complex feelings with ease and compassion.

It acts as a bridge, enabling us to traverse the divide between ourselves and others and to gain insight into people's perspectives. This means striving to understand the pain that underlies the actions of those who have caused us harm. While this doesn't justify their actions, it can foster compassion and open the path to forgiveness.

But empathy isn't solely about understanding others; it's also about understanding ourselves. To forgive ourselves, we must empathize with the emotions and motivations that may have contributed to our pain. This self-awareness is the key to healing and personal growth.

Empathy in forgiveness means finding a balance between understanding others and acknowledging our own emotions. It's important to validate our feelings while creating space for growth and ultimately letting go. However, this doesn't mean sacrificing our own well-being.

Cultivating Resilience Through Emotional Healing

Resilience is not a destination; it's a journey that starts with acknowledging your wounds, tending them with compassion, and emerging from the depths with newfound wisdom and strength. Emotional healing, the cornerstone of this journey, allows us to integrate our experiences, learn from our pain, and transform adversity into fuel for growth. We cultivate an inner fortitude that can weather any storm by facing our fears, exploring our vulnerabilities, and embracing our imperfections.

Through emotional healing, we bounce back from setbacks and thrive in the face of adversity. We learn to reframe challenges as opportunities, find meaning in our struggles, and harness our pain as a catalyst for personal growth. As we heal our emotional wounds, we strengthen our connection to ourselves and others, fostering deeper empathy, compassion, and understanding.

Resilience, born from your own emotional healing, is a gift you give yourself. It's a testament to the indomitable spirit within you, a beacon of hope that shines even in the darkest of times. By embracing the transformative power of emotional healing, you tap into your innate resilience, paving the way for a life of greater joy, meaning, and purpose.

CHAPTER 8

The Empathy Connection: Mirror Neurons and Understanding Others

"Empathy is seeing with the eyes of another, listening with the ears of another, and feeling with the heart of another."

- ALFRED ADLER

In the earlier chapter, we discussed emotions and how they affect our lives. In this chapter, we'll explore the concept of mirror neurons, which are special brain cells that fire when we perform an action and observe someone else doing the same. These cells help us understand and connect with others, which is what we call empathy.

The study of mirror neurons is a relatively new field of neuroscience, but it will be an exciting journey of discovery as we explore the science behind empathy and social awareness. We'll uncover some secrets and reveal some surprises along the way, so get ready to be amazed.

Biological Basis of Mirror Neurons

Mirror neurons are an incredible discovery in neuroscience. A team of scientists in Italy first identified them in the 1990s, and they have since fascinated researchers around the world.

So what exactly are mirror neurons? They're special cells in our brains that activate when we perform an action and when we watch someone else perform the same action. This process allows us to understand the actions, intentions, and emotions of others, and it's essential for social interaction.

For example, when we see someone smile, our mirror neurons activate as if we were smiling ourselves. This allows us to connect with their emotions and understand their feelings. Similarly, when we watch someone perform a task, our mirror neurons fire as if we were doing the same task ourselves. This can help us learn and improve our skills.

Interestingly, mirror neurons aren't unique to humans. Research has shown that other monkey species also have these neurons, which suggests that they may have developed early in primates to improve social communication and learning through imitation.

Although mirror neurons are fascinating, they're also incredibly complex. They rely on a combination of neurotransmitters and brain structures, including dopamine. Research shows that dopamine release can enhance our ability to learn from observed actions by reinforcing the connections between our neurons.

Unfortunately, some people may have difficulties with mirror neuron activity. For example, individuals with autism spectrum disorder (ASD) may have poor mirror neuron activity, making it harder for them to understand and copy social actions. Similarly, studies have suggested that individuals with schizophrenia may have altered mirror neuron function, which could contribute to their social cognitive problems.

Mirror neurons are an exciting area of research that can help us better understand ourselves and others. By studying these neurons, we can learn more about how we connect with the world around us and how we can improve our social interactions.

Chapter 8

Case Study of Mirror Neurons and Empathy

Mirror neurons activate both when an individual performs an action and when they observe another performing the same action. This has been a key focal point in the study of empathy. A compelling case study that illustrates this connection involves a young woman named Sarah, who suffered a traumatic brain injury in a car accident. Following her injury, Sarah exhibited a significant reduction in empathy, struggling to understand and respond to the emotions of others.

Brain imaging studies revealed damage to the regions of Sarah's brain associated with mirror neuron activity. This finding suggested a direct link between the impaired function of mirror neurons and her diminished capacity for empathy. Through rehabilitation therapy focused on reactivating these damaged neural pathways, Sarah gradually regained her ability to connect emotionally with others, providing further evidence for the role of mirror neurons in empathy.

Another intriguing aspect of this case study was the observation that Sarah's difficulty with empathy was not limited to emotional understanding. She also struggled with tasks that required her to anticipate the actions of others, suggesting that mirror neurons may play a broader role in social cognition beyond just empathy. This finding highlights the complex and multifaceted nature of empathy and the potential contributions of mirror neuron systems to our ability to understand and navigate the social world.

The mirror neurons provide insights into how we process social interactions. They encourage cooperation and coordination by allowing us to share representations of actions and experiences. For instance, seeing someone in pain triggers similar brain regions in the observer, resulting in a shared sense of discomfort.

Research has shown that some people may have difficulty understanding the emotions and intentions of others. This can be especially true for people with Autism Spectrum Disorder (ASD). Scientists believe that one probable reason for this is a problem with the "mirror neuron system" in the brain. These are special cells that help us understand what others are feeling and doing. If these cells don't work correctly, it can make social situations more difficult.

Although the exact role and mechanisms of mirror neurons are still being investigated, they undeniably shed light on how we perceive and relate to those around us. Their ability to simulate observed actions and emotions offers a biological basis for empathy, shaping our ability for connection and understanding. Further research into mirror neurons has the potential to deepen our comprehension of human relationships and our innate ability for compassion.

Role Of Mirror Neurons in Social Cognition

Mirror neurons offer a glimpse into the biological basis of social understanding. These cells fire when we perform an action and when we see someone else doing the same. This mirroring effect allows us to internally simulate the actions, intentions, and even the emotions of others.

Beyond simple actions, mirror neurons also play a role in emotional resonance. When we see someone experiencing joy, sadness, or other feelings, our mirror neurons can activate similarly, allowing us to share those emotions. This shared experience lays the foundation for empathy, helping us connect with others on a deeper level.

Furthermore, mirror neurons are crucial for learning through imitation. From an early age, we see and mimic the actions of others. This process helps us develop new skills, learn social cues, and integrate into our communities.

Chapter 8

The discovery of mirror neurons reveals a profound biological connection between observation, understanding, and empathy. They highlight the intricate link between watching someone's actions, feeling their emotions, and understanding their intentions – all of which are essential for navigating our complex social world.

Our journey through the world of mirror neurons has revealed a profound truth: the power of empathy allows us to connect with others on a deeply emotional level. We now understand that our brains are wired to resonate with the experiences of those around us, fostering a sense of shared humanity.

But what happens when the emotions we encounter are laced with pain or trauma? Can we navigate the complex landscape of memory and find a path toward healing and forgiveness? In our next chapter, "Memory and Forgiveness: Rewriting Painful Memories", we'll delve into the groundbreaking science of memory manipulation. We'll explore the intricate processes by which memories are formed and stored, and the surprising ways they can be modified.

CHAPTER 9

Memory and Forgiveness: Rewriting Painful Memories

> *"Forgiving does not erase the bitter past. A healed memory is not a deleted memory. Instead, forgiving what we cannot forget creates a new way to remember. We change the memory of our past into a hope for our future."*
>
> - Lewis B. Smedes

Have you ever struggled with painful memories or emotional wounds that seem to hold you back from moving forward? If so, you're not alone. In this chapter, we'll explore the power of the human mind to transform and heal, specifically through the acts of forgiveness and rewriting our stories.

We'll take a look at how forgiving others (and ourselves) can change the way we see our past, which allows us to grow and learn from it. We'll also examine how our memories shape our sense of self, and how we can use our capacity for forgiveness to heal old wounds and painful experiences.

By exploring these topics, we'll gain a better understanding of how our minds work, and how we can use this knowledge to change the way we think and feel. Whether you're struggling with past traumas or simply looking to grow as a person, this chapter will provide you with insights and tools to help you move forward and rewrite your own story.

Healing Through Reframing Traumatic Experiences

When it comes to healing from trauma, our memories can be incredibly powerful. They hold on to our pain and emotions, which can profoundly change our well-being. But we can transform our understanding of those memories by reframing them. This means questioning negative thoughts or beliefs that we may have developed about ourselves or others and replacing them with more balanced and compassionate interpretations of the events.

Reframing can offer a chance to find meaning and growth within adversity. Reframing extends to our relationships with others as well, as they often bear scars of resentment and betrayal. Therefore, it is crucial to approach these relationships with mutual understanding and empathy to foster healing. By viewing past actions with compassion, we regain personal power and create the potential for mending broken bonds.

Ultimately, reframing traumatic memories offers a profound path toward healing. By revisiting our pain and challenging negative beliefs, we can write a new narrative for ourselves. This process can help us let go of the weight of the past and create a brighter future filled with growth and happiness.

Rewriting Painful Memories: The Power of Empathy

Have you ever experienced a painful memory that seems to stick with you, making it hard to move on and forgive? The good news is that our innate ability to understand the feelings of others can help us change those memories.

By stepping back into those past experiences with empathy and grace, you can unravel the complex emotions tied to the painful memories. This allows you to view events from a different perspective. The goal is to see how our past experiences have influenced our reactions and recognize the circumstances that may have affected the actions of others.

The goal is to help us break free from the label of "victim" and acknowledge our pain without letting it define us. It's a journey of understanding—for ourselves and others—that breaks the cycle of pain. This process demands courage and patience, which ultimately leads to a happier and more peaceful life.

Similarly, empathy helps us nurture forgiveness toward those who have hurt us. Understanding the context of a person's actions—though not excusing them—can open a path toward understanding. This shift in perspective can loosen the grip of anger and resentment, creating the optimistic possibility for healing.

Therapeutic Techniques for Rewriting Traumatic Memories

Trauma can leave a lasting impact on our lives, manifesting as painful memories that can be difficult to shake off. Fortunately, several therapeutic techniques have proven effective in easing emotional distress and promoting personal growth.

One such technique is cognitive restructuring, which involves challenging negative thoughts and beliefs about a traumatic experience. By replacing self-blame with a more balanced and compassionate perspective, individuals can foster resilience and forgiveness.

Another technique is Eye Movement Desensitization and Reprocessing (EMDR), which stimulates both sides of the brain to reprocess trauma and experiences. This process reduces the emotional charge attached to memories, leading to a healthy and adaptive resolution.

Narrative therapy is another powerful tool that focuses on reframing our life's narratives in a positive light. By shifting our perspective from victimhood to strength, we can reclaim our agency and promote personal growth.

Mindfulness-based interventions teach individuals to see their thoughts and emotions without judgment, allowing them to detach from painful memories without becoming overwhelmed. By staying grounded in the present moment, individuals can practice self-compassion and forgiveness for the past.

These therapeutic techniques offer valuable tools for healing and personal growth. Whether it involves reprogramming our thoughts, reprocessing trauma, reshaping our life's narratives, or practicing mindfulness, the goal is to break free from the weight of the past and find peace and silence. By rewriting our painful memories, we empower ourselves to move forward and embrace a brighter future.

Emily's Transformation Through Reframing Trauma

Emily, a young graphic designer, faced a life-altering event when she was involved in a severe car accident. The trauma left her with chronic pain and a deep-seated fear of driving, which significantly impacted her daily life and career. Initially, Emily found herself trapped in a cycle of negative thoughts, reliving the accident repeatedly and allowing it to define her existence.

However, Emily's journey to healing began when she started attending therapy sessions focused on cognitive reframing. Her therapist introduced her to the concept of viewing her experience from a unique perspective. Instead of seeing the accident as a debilitating event, Emily learned to view it as a turning point that led to personal growth.

She began to appreciate the small victories, like the first time she could walk without pain or the moment she felt confident enough to get behind the wheel again. Emily reframed her experience by focusing on her resilience and the new paths that opened for her, such as her passion for advocating for road safety and supporting others who have gone through similar experiences.

Through the process of reframing, Emily transformed her traumatic experience into a source of strength. She no longer identified herself as a victim of the accident but rather as a survivor who overcame adversity. This shift in mindset allowed her to reclaim control over her life and find a deeper sense of purpose.

Emily was able to reframe her traumatic experience which led to profound personal transformation. By changing the narrative around a traumatic event, individuals like Emily can find healing and a renewed sense of self.

Assignment

I recommend using the same notebook or journal from earlier assignments. Here's an activity designed to promote healing by reframing traumatic experiences. It's best suited for those who are ready to explore their memories through a new lens.

The Reframing Activity

Purpose: To create a safe space to revisit a painful memory and actively reframe the associated thoughts, emotions, and perceptions.

Instructions:

1. Choose a Memory: Select a specific memory connected to your trauma that you feel ready to explore in a new light. It may be a single moment or an ongoing experience.

2. Initial Reflections:

    A. Briefly write about the memory: What happened? What were the circumstances surrounding the event(s)?

    B. Explore the emotions: How did this memory make you feel, both at the time and now? Use descriptive words to capture the intensity and complexity of your emotions.

    C. Identify current beliefs: What thoughts or beliefs do you have about yourself or others because of this memory? (Ex: "I am unlovable," "The world is unsafe," etc.)

3. The Reframing Process:

    A. Challenging negativity: With kindness toward yourself, begin to question the negative beliefs about yourself or others that you previously identified. Are these beliefs 100% true? Are there alternative explanations?

    B. Finding Growth: Can you find potential lessons or opportunities for growth within this memory? While painful, could it have taught you something about yourself or the world?

    C. Compassionate perspective: Imagine stepping outside of yourself and viewing the memory as a neutral observer. How might you interpret the actions or intentions of others? Is there room for a more understanding perspective?

    D. Rewriting the narrative: Create a short new "story" of the memory, incorporating your more balanced, compassionate insights. Focus on your strength, your resilience, and the potential for growth stemming from this experience.

4. Rewriting the narrative: Create a short new "story" of the memory, incorporating your more balanced, compassionate insights. Focus on your strength, your resilience, and the potential for growth stemming from this experience.

5. Reflection:

    A. How does this reframing process make you feel?

    B. What did you learn about yourself?

    C. Is there any shift in perspective, even just a small one?

Important Notes:

- **Go at your own pace.** This process takes time; be gentle with yourself. If certain emotions feel overwhelming, pause and practice grounding techniques (deep breathing, etc.).

- **Seek support.** This activity is best done alongside a therapist for guidance and support. Discuss your entries with them for deeper processing.

- **Celebrate progress.** Acknowledge even small shifts in how you perceive your traumatic experiences. Reframing is a journey, and every step toward healing is worth celebrating.

Forgiveness can be a powerful tool that can help us cope with traumatic experiences. By trying to understand others, forgiving ourselves, engaging with collective memories, and possibly seeking support from therapy if needed, we can turn our pain into strength. This process doesn't erase the past, but it helps us change the way we see it, making us stronger and more hopeful.

Moreover, forgiving oneself is crucial in breaking free from self-destructive narratives that perpetuate pain and suffering. Through self-compassion and acceptance, individuals can transform their internal dialogue into one that promotes healing and resilience.

As we continue exploring the path of forgiveness, it's important to understand the profound role our subconscious mind plays. Could unresolved emotions lingering beneath the surface be disrupting our sleep and hindering our ability to truly heal? In our next chapter, "Forgiveness and Sleep: The Role of the Subconscious Mind", we'll delve into this fascinating connection and uncover the secrets of achieving deeper healing and restorative rest.

CHAPTER 10

Forgiveness and Sleep: The Role of the Subconscious Mind

> *"Sleep deprivation is an illegal torture method outlawed by the Geneva Convention and international law, but most of us do it to ourselves."*
>
> - RYAN HURD

Harnessing the potential of your subconscious mind to facilitate healing and personal growth involves liberating oneself from the constraints of conscious thinking. The subconscious communicates with us through dreams, symbols, and metaphors, circumventing the limitations of logic and rationale.

Therefore, as you prepare to embrace sleep, remain receptive and open-hearted, for it is within the realm of dreams that genuine forgiveness has the potential to unfold. The subconscious mind is a captivating facet of our existence that psychologists have long sought to comprehend. It represents a concealed force that significantly impacts our mental and emotional well-being. This section delves into the interconnectedness of forgiveness and sleep, unraveling how the subconscious mind facilitates our journey toward healing and personal development.

Importance of Sleep on Forgiveness

Sleep is essential for our mental and emotional health; it's not a luxury but a biological necessity. Research has shown that when we are well-rested, we think more clearly and manage difficult emotions better. On the other hand, sleep deprivation leaves us feeling anxious, irritable, and less equipped to navigate challenging situations, making it harder to find the empathy necessary for forgiveness. This can make it especially difficult to process the anger or frustration accompanying past hurts.

But a good night's rest provides the emotional bandwidth we need to approach this complex process. Emotional bandwidth refers to our capacity to manage and process emotions.

Sleep also unlocks the depths of our subconscious mind, where unresolved emotions often exist. During sleep, our brain merges memories, integrates experiences, and regulates our emotional responses. All these processes are vital for navigating the process of forgiveness.

When we're awake, our memories of hurt and pain may remain fragmented, making it difficult to understand their full impact. Sleep allows our brains to piece together these fragments, connecting them to other experiences and knowledge. This process gives us a deeper understanding of our emotions, helping us make sense of the pain and begin to heal.

During Rapid Eye Movement (REM) sleep, the stage characterized by vivid dreams, our brains work even harder at processing emotions. Key emotion-related areas like the amygdala and prefrontal cortex become highly active. This allows us to dive even deeper into the complex feelings surrounding forgiveness while in a safe, subconscious state.

The power of sleep, through its impact on memory consolidation and emotional regulation, gradually helps us unravel buried emotions. By accessing the wisdom of our subconscious minds during sleep, we gain the understanding and clarity needed to process pain, let go of resentment, and ultimately forgive. Embracing sleep's power truly supports our journey toward forgiveness and emotional healing.

Chapter 10

To ensure good sleep habits, try these tips:

- Maintain a consistent sleep schedule. Aim to go to bed and wake up at the same time each day.

- Create a relaxing bedtime routine. Wind down with calming activities like reading or taking a warm bath.

- Optimize your sleep environment. Keep your bedroom dark, quiet, and at a comfortable temperature.

- Avoid caffeine and electronic devices before bed. These can disrupt your natural sleep patterns.

By prioritizing sleep, you give yourself the emotional resilience and mental clarity needed to navigate the complexities of forgiveness.

Unconscious Healing Through the Subconscious Mind

One intriguing aspect of the subconscious mind is its ability to provide unconscious healing, particularly about forgiveness. This phenomenon occurs when we enter a state of deep sleep, and our conscious mind gradually fades away, allowing our subconsciousness to take control. It is through our subconsciousness that memories long forgotten resurface, demanding our attention. Our past experiences are woven together with our emotions, creating a tapestry that can lead to forgiveness.

The subconscious mind communicates with us through dreams and symbols, using a language that is abstract yet deeply meaningful. These dreams may contain vivid images or scenarios that reflect our unresolved conflicts or lingering resentments. By exploring these dreamscapes with an open heart and a readiness to confront our innermost fears and insecurities, we can start the process of forgiveness.

Unconscious healing can occur on different emotional, psychological, and physical levels. During sleep, our subconscious mind navigates through complex paths, gradually untangling knots formed by past emotional wounds. Releasing pent-up emotions through catharsis can cleanse deep-seated pain and resentment.

Recent research has revealed the physiological changes that happen in our bodies while we are asleep, which aid in unconscious healing. Neurotransmitters and hormones are released during sleep, promoting relaxation and cellular repair. This biological rejuvenation not only contributes to our overall well-being but also plays a crucial role in the healing process helped by the subconscious mind.

In short, the subconscious mind has an innate capacity for unconscious healing, particularly when it comes to forgiveness. By surrendering control to the enigmatic realm of dreams and symbols, we open ourselves up to a transformative journey that can lead us toward emotional liberation. As we embrace this mysterious process with open hearts and minds, we can unlock the potential for profound personal growth and healing that lies dormant within us all.

How Forgiveness Impacts Dream Content

Exploring forgiveness within the context of dream content is a fascinating psychological and neurocognitive research intersection. Forgiveness can profoundly influence one's emotional state and cognitive processes, which are reflected in dreams' content. Academic research suggests that forgiveness may restructure dream narratives, shifting them from hostility and aggression to reconciliation and peace themes.

When an individual harbors unforgiveness, it can manifest as recurring themes of conflict and distress within their dreams. Conversely, forgiveness can transform these dreamscapes, potentially leading to more positive and less aggressive dream content.

Furthermore, the content of dreams post-forgiveness may also reflect the cognitive processing of forgiveness itself. Dreams could serve as a mental rehearsal space where the forgiving individual explores scenarios of empathy, understanding, and compassion, which may not only aid in combining these new perspectives but also contribute to the reinforcement of the forgiving attitude in waking life.

Psychological Benefits of Integrating Forgiveness and Sleep

Forgiveness and sleep are two of the most powerful weapons in our arsenal to combat stress, anxiety, and depression. By forgiving, we let go of negative emotions that can disrupt our sleep, leading to overall mental well-being. This cycle is the key to emotional regulation and building healthier relationships based on trust and understanding.

To prioritize forgiveness, we need to understand the importance of sleep. Sleep allows our minds and bodies to process complex emotions, including those that are associated with past hurts. This process strengthens our emotional resilience, making it easier to approach forgiveness with compassion and understanding. When we forgive, we experience a reduction in stress, anxiety, and depression, which can lead to better sleep. This harmonious cycle further promotes mental clarity, inner peace, and the ability to tackle the challenges of forgiveness with greater strength and clarity.

CHAPTER 11

Confronting the Pain Without Being Overwhelmed

"You don't have to control your thoughts. You just have to stop letting them control you."

- Dan Millman

Emotional pain can be daunting, looming over you and casting a long shadow on your happiness. The thought of climbing it, of facing those raw emotions head-on, might seem overwhelming. But here's the secret: dodging the mountain won't make it disappear. Avoiding your pain allows it to fester, eventually spilling over and impacting other areas of your life.

Confronting emotional pain, however, is an act of incredible strength. It's like taking the first step toward a breathtaking summit. By acknowledging your pain and exploring its source, you gain the power to understand it. This understanding becomes your toolkit for navigating the climb. You'll discover healthy coping mechanisms, build resilience, and ultimately find the path to a brighter, more fulfilling future. Remember, conquering your emotional mountain is not about reaching the top instantly but about taking the first brave step and finding the strength to keep climbing.

Facing the Hurt

Addressing the pain head-on requires courage. It's about peering into the shadows and recognizing the hurt for what it is—a part of our experience, but not the entirety of who we are. To do this without being overwhelmed, consider these approaches:

- **Name Your Pain.** Sometimes, simply putting a name to what you're feeling can diminish the power it holds over you. Are you angry, disappointed, betrayed? Identifying your emotions gives you a starting point for addressing them.
- **Detach with Love.** Practice seeing your pain as if you were an outsider looking in. This isn't about disowning your feelings but about giving yourself the compassion and understanding you'd offer a friend in distress.

Balancing Act

The line between confronting pain and being hurt again can be thin. The key is finding a balance that allows you to acknowledge your hurt without reliving it in a way that causes further harm. Strategies for striking this balance include:

- **Setting Emotional Boundaries.** Decide in advance how deeply you'll delve into your feelings at any given time. It's okay to say, "This is as far as I go today."
- **Safe Spaces.** Choose a specific location where you feel secure to explore your feelings. This could be a quiet room in your home, a spot in nature, or any place that offers comfort and solitude.

Small Steps

Moving toward healing is a process that receives help from a gentle, gradual approach. Taking small, manageable steps can prevent you from becoming overwhelmed and help maintain your resilience. Implement this strategy by:

- **Timed Reflections.** Allocate a brief, set amount of time each day to reflect on your feelings. Limiting this time prevents spiraling into negative thought patterns.

- **Controlled Exposure.** If writing or speaking about your pain, do so in controlled doses. You might start by writing a few sentences or sharing a brief thought with a confidante, gradually increasing as you feel more comfortable.

Support Systems

The value of a robust support system cannot be overstated. Friends, family, and professionals can offer not just comfort but also perspective that is sometimes lost when we're deep in our pain. Lean on these supports by:

- **Sharing Selectively.** Choose to share your feelings with those who have shown understanding and empathy in the past. They're likely to offer the support you need during this time.

- **Professional Guidance.** Sometimes, the insight and techniques provided by a therapist or counselor can be invaluable. They can offer strategies tailored to your specific situation, helping you navigate your feelings in a healthy way.

Facing our pain directly is a daunting task, yet it's one that holds the promise of true healing. By naming our hurt, setting boundaries, taking small steps, and leaning on our support systems, we can acknowledge our pain without letting it overwhelm us. This approach not only fosters resilience but also paves the way for a deeper, more meaningful process of forgiveness.

Make A Difference with your Review

"Holding on is believing that there's only a past; letting go is knowing that there's a future."

- **Daphne Rose Kingma**

Be The Change With Just A Few Clicks

Imagine if a few taps on your screen could ignite a positive change. What if your words had the power to inspire, uplift, and help someone? This isn't just wishful thinking – it's the real impact your book review can have!

My mission is to make the benefits of forgiveness accessible to everyone. And the only way for me to carry out that mission is by reaching... well, everyone.

This is where you come in. Most people do, in fact, judge a book by its cover (and its reviews). So here's my ask on behalf of someone who may need a gentle push to start their journey toward a better life.

Please help them by leaving this book a review.

Your help (in the form of a review) costs no money and takes less than 60 seconds to make real, but it can change a person's mental health and life forever

Chapter 11

Click the link below or scan the QR code.

Submit your review and know you may have helped someone to a healthier, happier world.

https://www.amazon.com/review/review-your- purchases/?asin= B0CTNTCK6S

Thank you for choosing to make a difference.

With gratitude and warmth, J.J. Nicolls

CHAPTER 12

The Art of Self-forgiveness: Neurological Pathways to Inner Peace

"How unhappy is he who cannot forgive himself."
- Publilius Syrus

Self-forgiveness is a tool that can bring you inner peace and well-being. It enables you to treat yourself with kindness and learn from your mistakes. Practicing self-forgiveness can help you replace negative thoughts with positive ones and create new neural pathways in your brain. Recent studies have shown that our brains can heal and forgive ourselves, making this process even more powerful.

This chapter will explain in detail self-forgiveness and how it can rewire how your brain processes emotions. Understanding the science behind self-forgiveness can empower you to let go of past wounds and move forward with a renewed sense of purpose and self-love.

Definition Of Self-Forgiveness and Its Benefits

Self-forgiveness can be challenging. Yet it is a crucial step for personal growth and happiness. This involves taking responsibility for our mistakes, recognizing our imperfections, and freeing ourselves from any negative emotions associated with them. It's not about making excuses or avoiding consequences. Instead, it's about recognizing our mistakes and allowing ourselves the opportunity to move forward in a positive direction. When we practice self-forgiveness, we can release any guilt or shame that may hamper our progress for a more promising future.

One key aspect is understanding that everyone makes mistakes. No one is perfect, and expecting yourself to be flawless in every aspect of your life is unrealistic. By recognizing this fact, we can instead focus on learning from our mistakes and growing as individuals.

It will require taking complete responsibility for our actions. We must recognize the harm we have caused ourselves or others and take necessary steps to make amends. Understanding our role in causing harm is the first step toward healing.

Forgiving yourself is a powerful tool that helps us let go of self-blame and allows us to move forward with peace. It is important to remember that self-forgiveness also enables us to cultivate self-compassion. We will develop greater compassion for others when we show compassion toward ourselves, even when we have made mistakes. This increased empathy helps us navigate tricky situations with grace and understanding.

Inner absolution is vital in promoting a profound sense of self-worth and confidence. By forgiving ourselves for our past mistakes, we can recognize our value beyond those errors and significantly elevate our confidence levels. This newfound self-worth empowers us to embrace new challenges without fear or hesitation.

By embracing ourselves, we can move forward in life with a greater sense of peace, self-love, and acceptance. Remember that you are worthy of self-forgiveness and that it's okay to make mistakes.

Self-Forgiveness VS Seeking Forgiveness from Others

Forgiving oneself and seeking forgiveness from someone else are two important processes that can help us feel better about ourselves and our relationships. When we forgive ourselves, it requires acknowledging past wrongdoings, accepting responsibility where appropriate, and making a conscious decision to move forward with self-compassion. The process of self-forgiveness centers on releasing shame, guilt, and self-recrimination, which can hinder personal growth.

On the other hand, when we seek forgiveness from someone else, it means we want to make things right after we have hurt them. This process can help repair our relationships and build trust. It involves apologizing for what we did wrong, showing we are sorry, and asking for their forgiveness. Even if they don't forgive us right away, trying to make amends can show that we care about the relationship and are willing to work on it.

Importance of Taking Responsibility for One's Actions

Are you ready to move forward with renewed energy and a sense of purpose? Let's tap into your self-awareness and unlock your full potential together! Achieving true self-forgiveness requires an understanding of personal responsibility. While forgiveness ultimately involves releasing self-blame and practicing self-compassion, it should not be confused with completely avoiding responsibility for one's past actions. Acknowledging personal responsibility is a critical foundation for authentic self-forgiveness and subsequent personal growth.

Assuming responsibility as part of self-forgiveness requires a precise balance. It demands confronting earlier errors or detrimental behaviors without spiraling into a pattern of extreme self-blame. This approach enables us to pinpoint the precise choice that resulted in harm to either ourselves or to others. By understanding the origins of our depravities, we set up the basis for authentic change that goes beyond mere wishful thinking.

Responsibility also empowers us on our journey toward self-forgiveness. Owning our actions, as uncomfortable as they may be, grants us agency. Recognizing that while past behaviors cannot be changed, we can actively choose a different path forward.

Authentic self-forgiveness that incorporates genuine responsibility offers profound benefits. It releases us from the debilitating weight of excessive guilt and shame, promotes psychological well-being, and strengthens our ability for self-improvement

Decoding Self-Reflection: Your Brain's Guide to Healing

Neural networks play a crucial role in self-reflection, especially when it comes to self-forgiveness. These networks are made up of complex systems of interconnected neurons in the prefrontal cortex, amygdala, and hippocampus. Their main function is to process information, make connections, and form memories related to our past actions and emotions. When we engage in self-reflection, these neural networks are activated, allowing us to examine our thoughts and feelings about ourselves and our past behaviors.

The process of self-reflection, a cornerstone of self-awareness, is a fascinating area of study that also serves as a conduit for mental healing. Thanks to cognitive neuroscience, we now have a deeper understanding of how this introspective activity is facilitated by a distinct brain network that processes self-related information. Moran (2016) offers a unique insight, elaborating that self-reflection activates a superordinate cognitive schema, indicating that our brains encode self-related information differently from other types of information. This schema and the associated brain network, which includes areas active during rest and mind-wandering, are key to understanding ourselves and our place in the world.

Further research by Herwig et al. (2012) delves into the neural activity that underpins self-reflection, revealing that it involves increased activation in the dorsomedial and lateral prefrontal cortex, insula, and anterior and posterior cingulate cortex. These areas, known for their involvement in self-monitoring and self-regulation, underscore their significance in the brain's self-healing aspects. This research not only deepens our understanding of self-reflection but also opens avenues for potential therapeutic interventions.

Several research studies have also shown that self-forgiveness can lead to positive changes in brain activity. A study conducted by researchers at Stanford University found that participants who practiced meditation showed increased brain activity in areas associated with empathy and compassion. This is proof that self-forgiveness not only enhances our mental well-being but also has a significant positive impact on our social interactions and relationships.

CHAPTER 13

Navigating Your Forgiveness Roadmap

"All you need is the plan, the road map, and the courage to press on to your destination."

- EARL NIGHTINGALE

Imagine standing beautiful landscape, with the path ahead of you winding toward the horizon where the future awaits. This path is the journey of forgiveness, which can be challenging but ultimately liberating. To navigate this path, you need to have a sense of direction and a map and understand that you are in control of your journey. It's not about rushing toward the end but taking in the scenery, overcoming obstacles, and gaining strength with every step. Your resilience is your greatest asset and will guide you through this journey.

Forgiveness is not a straightforward process but a journey with ups and downs. Recognizing this complexity is the first step toward making the process easier and less frustrating. Let's explore the different stages of forgiveness, set realistic expectations, and develop strategies to help you overcome obstacles. Remember that many have walked this path before you; their experiences can help you by reminding you that you are not alone.

The Stages of Forgiveness: A Roadmap

Forgiveness unfolds in stages, each with its own landscape and challenges. Identifying these stages helps us navigate the process with a clearer understanding of where we are and where we're heading.

Initial Pain:

The point of impact where the pain is fresh and raw. Here emotions run high, and forgiveness might seem impossible.

Feelings:

- Shock: A sense of disbelief and disorientation as the world feels suddenly out of alignment.
- Anger: Intense rage and a desire for retribution.
- Sadness: Overwhelming feelings of loss, disappointment, and despair.
- Betrayal: Deep wound of violated trust, especially if the hurt came from someone close.
- Confusion: Difficulty processing what happened and making sense of the situation.
- Fear: Anxiety about the future, vulnerability, and the possibility of the pain recurring.

Challenges:

- Emotional Regulation: Managing the intensity of the emotions is incredibly difficult, often leading to outbursts or unhealthy coping mechanisms.
- Impulsivity: The desire for immediate revenge or lashing out can be strong.
- Black-and-White Thinking: Seeing the situation in stark terms of good vs. evil, with little room for nuance.
- Isolation: Pulling away from others out of shame, fear of judgment, or simply feeling overwhelmed.

- Physical Manifestations: Emotional pain can manifest as physical symptoms; sleep disturbances, headaches, appetite changes, etc.

Understanding:

Striving to see the situation from a broader perspective. This might include considering the offender's motivations, though not excusing their actions.

Feelings:

- Curiosity: A desire to understand the "why" behind the hurtful behavior.
- Open-Mindedness: A willingness to consider new perspectives.
- Ambivalence: Conflicting emotions of empathy and lingering resentment.
- Relief: Gaining insights can bring a sense of relief.
- Connection: Recognizing shared human flaws can foster a surprising sense of connection, even amidst the pain.

Challenges:

- Self-Blame: The trap of wondering if you somehow contributed to the hurtful behavior.
- Excusing Behavior: Understanding motivations must be carefully balanced with holding the person accountable for harmful actions.
- Emotional Resistance: Your pain may cloud your ability to view the situation with any objectivity.
- Lack of Information: Sometimes, understanding is hindered by not having access to the other person's thoughts or the full context of their actions.

- Fear: Probing deeper may raise fears of discovering further pain.

Compassion and Empathy:

Beginning to feel compassion for oneself and, possibly, for the offender. This stage is where the heart starts to soften.

Feelings:

- Understanding: A shift from feeling solely victimized to recognizing the human struggles and possible motivations behind the hurtful actions (this does NOT mean excusing the behavior).
- Perspective: The ability to see the event within a broader context, potentially considering contributing factors like past trauma or mental health issues.
- Conflict: While feelings of compassion appear, there is still anger and hurt.
- Curiosity: A willingness to explore the other person's world, without losing sight of your pain.
- Compassion for Self: Recognizing your suffering and deservingness of kindness.

Challenges:

- Justifying Behavior: It's crucial to distinguish between understanding motivations and condoning harmful actions.
- Self-Betrayal: Fear that compassion somehow diminishes your own pain or experience.
- Moral Dilemma: Feeling like forgiving "bad" behavior is wrong or goes against deeply held values.

- Judgment: Struggling with judgmental thoughts toward oneself ("I should be further along") or the other person ("they don't deserve empathy").

Acknowledgment:

Recognizing and accepting the hurt without minimizing or exaggerating it. This stage involves facing the pain head-on.

Feelings:

- Shock and Disbelief: The realization of the hurt can be deeply disorienting.
- Overwhelm: Emotional flooding is common, with intense surges of anger, sadness, fear, and confusion.
- Betrayal: A sense of broken trust.
- Vulnerability: Facing your pain can feel incredibly exposing.
- Desire for Revenge: Thoughts of wanting the other person to suffer may arise, which can later feed into feelings of guilt or shame.

Challenges:

- Avoidance: Denying or numbing the pain often through unhealthy coping mechanisms.
- Self-Blame: Internalizing the hurt or questioning if you somehow brought it on yourself.
- Rumination: Replaying the events and agonizing over the event.
- Isolation: Feeling ashamed or afraid to share the experience, leading to withdrawal.

- Difficulty with Daily Life: The raw emotional distress can make focusing on everyday tasks challenging.

Release:

Letting go of the anger, bitterness, or desire for retribution. It's a pivotal moment that often feels like a weight has been lifted.

Feelings:

- Relief: The burden of resentment begins to fade.
- Freedom: Less pull toward the past.
- Empowerment: Ability to choose to let go of negativity
- Peace: A sense of calm and a reduction of anger or hurt.
- Possibility: Hope for a more positive outlook.

Challenges:

- Self-Doubt: Questions whether this release is genuine or sustainable.
- Lingering Resentment: Old feelings may resurface.
- Fear of Vulnerability: A worry about being hurt again.
- False Expectations: Release doesn't mean instant happiness or forgetting what happened.

Reconstruction:

Rebuilding and moving forward, whether that includes the offender or not. This stage involves setting healthy boundaries and possibly redefining relationships.

Feelings:

- Strength: A sense of ability to take control of your own well-being.

- Resilience: Confidence in your ability to bounce back.
- Cautious Optimism: Rekindled hope for healthier relationships.
- Self-Respect: Increased sense of worthiness and respect for yourself.

Challenges:

- Redefining Boundaries: Determining appropriate levels of contact, emotional investment, and trust.
- Vulnerability: Allowing yourself to trust again.
- Letting Go of Control: Accepting that you can't dictate the other person's behavior or growth.
- Grief: Grief that the relationship can't be salvaged.
- Adjustment Period: Adapting to new dynamics in the relationship (if any) may take time and patience

Peace and Closure:

Finding a sense of peace and closure, marking the end of the forgiveness process.

Feelings:

- Relief: A sense of releasing a heavy emotional burden.
- Calmness: Reduced anger and preoccupation with the past.
- Empowerment: The realization that forgiveness is a choice.
- Gratitude: Appreciation for the lessons learned and personal growth achieved.
- Hope: Renewed optimism for the future.

Challenges:

- Lingering Traces: Fleeting moments of sadness or anger
- Doubt: There might be a nagging fear that the hurt could reoccur.
- Shifting Identity: If the hurt was a core part of how you saw yourself, finding a new, more positive self-narrative takes time.
- Relationship Dynamics: Forgiveness doesn't guarantee the relationship can be mended.

Samantha's Path to Serenity

Samantha's world was turned upside down when she discovered her business partner, whom she considered a second sister, had embezzled funds from their joint venture. The initial pain was devastating, and the betrayal shook the very foundation of her trust.

As the initial shock subsided, Samantha sought understanding. She delved into the circumstances that led to the embezzlement. She discovered that her partner had a gambling problem, and out of fear of losing the home where she and her child lived, she took the money. This insight didn't excuse the actions, but it illuminated the human weakness behind them.

With a heavy heart, Samantha embraced compassion and empathy. She reflected on the pressures of their business, the personal struggles her partner faced, and how a gambling addiction can lead to poor choices. Her empathy bridged the gap between anger and the possibility of forgiveness.

The stage of acknowledgment was a pivotal moment. Samantha reached out to her partner, and they faced the painful reality of the situation together. It was a conversation filled with tears, regret, and a mutual desire to heal the wounds that she felt.

Samantha found comfort in meditation and journaling; each day of work for forgiveness brought her a step closer to releasing the past. This process took her 10 months times, but reconstruction was a time of rebuilding, not just the business but the trust that had been shattered. Samantha and her partner implemented new checks and balances, ensuring transparency and accountability in their business.

At last, Samantha arrived at peace. It was a state of grace, born from the turmoil of betrayal and the hard work of forgiveness. She found peace knowing she had navigated the storm and emerged stronger, wiser, and more compassionate.

Samantha's journey was a testament to the power of forgiveness, a process that mended her relationship and led to profound self-discovery and personal growth.

Navigating Setbacks

Setbacks are part of the journey. They're not signs of failure but opportunities for deeper understanding and growth.

- **Expect and Accept.** Know that setbacks are likely. Accepting this reality can make them less discouraging when they occur.
- **Reflect and Learn.** Use setbacks as chances to reflect on what triggered them and how you can navigate similar situations in the future.
- **Support Network.** Lean on friends, family, or a therapist for support. Sometimes, an outside perspective can offer clarity and comfort.

Forgiveness is a complex, deeply personal process that unfolds in its own time. Understanding its stages, setting realistic expectations, and developing strategies for patience and setbacks can make the journey smoother and more meaningful.

The Power of Acknowledgment

In the realm of healing, the act of acknowledging one's feelings is transformative. It's comparable to turning on a light in a previously darkened room, allowing us to see and understand the contours of our emotional landscape. This illumination brings into focus the hurt, anger, and perhaps even a sense of betrayal that we've harbored, validating their existence and their impact on our lives. Such acknowledgment is not about dwelling in our pain but rather recognizing it as a critical step on the path to liberation from it.

Validating our emotions serves as an affirmation of our experiences. It paves the way for a deeper understanding of ourselves and the situations that have caused us pain. And acknowledgment is the first step in transforming our relationship with our emotions, from one of avoidance and suppression to one of acceptance and understanding.

Assignment on "If I'm Facing Pain... Tools for Finding Your Way"

Introduction: Facing the pain that comes with forgiveness can be daunting. These "if" scenarios can help you choose healthy strategies tailored to your needs at any given moment. There's no right or wrong way to utilize these tools – trust your instincts.

Scenarios:

1) IF... the initial pain feels overwhelming, I can:

    a) Option 1: Focus on my breath, even just 5 slow inhales/exhales.

    b) Option 2: Name one physical thing I can feel/see/hear right now to ground myself.

    c) Option 3: _____ (add your own coping tool)

2) IF... I can't put a name to my emotions, I can:

    a) Option 1: Draw or scribble how I feel, focusing on color/shape, not making it "art."

    b) Option 2: Find a song that matches my mood, let myself fully feel it while listening.

    c) Option 3: _____ (add your own)

3) IF... I feel like I'm being sucked back into the pain, I can:

    a) Option 1: Set a timer for 5 minutes of feeling it, then I MUST take a break.

    b) Option 2: Physically distance myself from where I am (move to a different room, etc.)

    c) Option 3: _____ (add your own)

4) IF... I need a safe space to process, I can:

    a) Option 1: Go to _____ (a specific location that feels comforting)

    b) Option 2: Talk to _____ (a trusted person, therapist if you have one)

    c) Option 3: _____ (add your own)

Chapter 13

5) IF... I'm afraid this pain will never end, I can:

   a) Option 1: Remind myself that emotions are waves, they rise and fall naturally.

   b) Option 2: Identify even ONE small positive change since the initial hurt.

   c) Option 3: _____ (add your own)

Additional Notes Section:

It's OK to use a tool repeatedly if it's working for you at that time. As you heal, the tools you need will likely change. That's GOOD! If an 'if' scenario isn't helpful, just skip it. This is about what works for YOU.

CHAPTER 14

Seeking Professional Help: When to Consider Therapy

"Asking for help isn't a sign of weakness, it's a sign of strength."
- MICHELLE OBAMA

In the landscape of healing and forgiveness, reaching out for professional help can be likened to finding a guide when we've lost our way in unfamiliar territory. This guide doesn't walk the path for us but shines a light on the hidden markers and milestones we might have missed, helping us move forward confidently and clearly.

Recognizing the Need

The decision to seek therapy is a deeply personal one, often coming at a crossroads where internal resources seem insufficient to overcome the hurdles we face. Signals that professional support could be beneficial might include:

- Persistent feelings of sadness, anger, or depression that don't improve over time.

- A sense of being stuck, where the weight of the past hurts stays unyielding despite your best efforts.

- Experiencing symptoms of anxiety, such as constant worry or physical manifestations like insomnia or fatigue, which are linked to the issues you're struggling to forgive.

- Your emotional state overwhelmingly impacts finding relationships, work, or daily life.
- Acknowledging these signs isn't an admission of defeat but rather a recognition of your strength and willingness to take active steps toward healing.

The Role of Therapy

If you've been carrying a heavy burden for too long and it's wearing you down, I want you to know that therapy can provide you with a much-needed source of relief and support. You'll have a safe and confidential environment where you can explore your thoughts, emotions, and behaviors with a compassionate and highly trained professional who genuinely cares about your well-being. Therapy can help you find ways to cope with your struggles and provide you with practical tools to make lasting changes in your life. Don't hesitate to reach out for help if you need it.

It is a journey that will help you gain insights into the root causes of your struggles, develop coping mechanisms, and learn strategies for managing difficult emotions. You'll feel empowered to break free from harmful patterns and build a life that is more aligned with your values, making you feel stronger and more capable.

It is important to remember that seeking therapy isn't a sign of weakness; it's a courageous act of self-investment. You deserve to have someone who can help you navigate your challenges and provide the tools you need to manage future ones independently. Think of therapy as learning a new language - the language of your mind and emotions. Through treatment, you'll gain fluency in understanding yourself better, fostering greater self-compassion, healthy communication skills, and a toolkit for emotional well-being that you can carry with you for the rest of your life.

Chapter 14

Traditional Types of Therapeutic Approaches

The therapy field is rich with diverse approaches, each offering unique benefits. When considering therapy, it might be helpful to explore:

- Cognitive-Behavioral Therapy (CBT) focuses on identifying and changing negative thought and behavior patterns. CBT is particularly effective for addressing depression and anxiety that might go with the forgiveness process.

- Narrative Therapy emphasizes the stories we tell about our lives and seeks to reframe these narratives to empower the individual. This approach can help those struggling to redefine their identity after being hurt.

- Trauma-Informed Therapy is specifically designed to address the effects of trauma, creating a safe and supportive environment for healing. It's ideal for individuals whose forgiveness challenges stem from traumatic experiences.

- Psychodynamic Therapy explores unconscious processes and past experiences related to current behavior and emotions. This approach can uncover deep-seated reasons for the difficulty in forgiving, offering insights that pave the way for healing.

Choosing the right approach depends on your individual experiences, the specific issues you have, and what feels most comfortable for you. A good therapist will work with you to find the most effective path.

Technology and Forgiveness

Treatment can be a difficult and personal journey, but you don't have to go it alone. Nowadays, more and more people are turning to technology for help and guidance on their path toward forgiveness. It's incredible how much support and assistance you can find through the power of modern technology.

- Online Therapy Sessions can provide you with convenient, one-on-one guidance to help you work through the complexities of forgiveness, especially for those in remote areas or with busy schedules.

- Social Media, when used correctly, can foster a sense of belonging and shared experiences, which can deepen our comprehension and understanding toward those who look to forgive.

- Virtual Support Groups can offer a safe and accessible space for sharing and validation in knowing that you're not alone on your path toward healing.

By embracing the potential of technology, we can unlock new possibilities for healing and growth. These tools offer a powerful reminder that forgiveness is possible, and we don't have to walk the path alone.

Overcoming Stigma

Despite growing awareness of mental health, some still feel stigmatized by seeking therapy. It's vital to remember that reaching out for help signifies strength, resilience, and a proactive stance toward one's well-being. Therapy is a tool, much like education or physical training, which enhances one's ability to navigate life's challenges.

Remember, seeking therapy is an act of self-care, no different from visiting a doctor for physical ailments. Consider starting with a single session. There's no commitment to continue if it doesn't feel right, but it might be the first step toward significant change.

Chapter 14

Talk about your decision with trusted friends or family who can provide support. Often, you'll find others who have benefitted from therapy themselves.

Choosing to seek professional help in the forgiveness process is a courageous act of self-compassion. It's about recognizing when your weight requires more than you can manage alone and being open to the guidance and support that can help lighten the load. Therapy offers a way forward through the knowledge of those skilled in navigating the difficult terrain of emotional healing.

CHAPTER 15

Moving Forward after Forgiveness: Setting Boundaries, Self-care, and Gratitude

"Self-care is how you take your power back."
- Lalah Delia

Moving forward after forgiveness can be a difficult and emotional journey. It is entirely normal to feel overwhelmed during this time. Please remember that taking care of yourself should always be your top priority. This chapter is dedicated to helping you set healthy boundaries, prioritize self-care, and practice gratitude.

To foster this resilience requires a focus on positivity. Try intentionally choosing positive interactions, as this can shift your perspective and bring hope and optimism. This, in turn, can lead to healthier relationship dynamics.

Importance of Setting Healthy Boundaries

Setting healthy boundaries is crucial for keeping emotional well-being and fostering positive relationships. Boundaries function as a protective barrier, preventing others from overstepping or taking advantage of us. When we establish clear boundaries, we communicate our needs and expectations to others, creating a sense of respect and understanding in our interactions. Without them, we may find ourselves feeling overwhelmed, resentful, or drained by the demands of others. Setting healthy boundaries allows us to prioritize our own needs and values, ensuring that we are not sacrificing our well-being for the sake of pleasing others.

Moreover, setting healthy boundaries empowers us to take control of our lives and make choices that align with our values and priorities. By clearly defining what is acceptable and unacceptable behavior in our relationships, we can avoid situations that compromise our integrity or make us feel uncomfortable. Boundaries help us have a sense of self-respect and self-worth, enabling us to assert ourselves confidently in various situations. When we set boundaries with others, we are asserting our right to be treated with dignity and respect, which is essential for supporting healthy relationships.

Boundaries: Protecting Your Progress

In a world that often pushes us to our limits, understanding and setting healthy boundaries is not just an act of self-preservation and self-respect, but a powerful tool for enhancing our mental well-being, improving relationships, and developing self-awareness and self-respect. Boundaries define what you're okay with and what you're not, encompassing your physical and emotional space, your time, energy, and how you want to be treated by others.

Why Boundaries Matter

- **Mental Health Shield.** Clear boundaries safeguard your mental well-being, preventing resentment, burnout, and depleting your emotional reserves.

- **Relationship Roadmap.** Boundaries are the unspoken 'rules of engagement' for every relationship in our lives, from romantic partners to coworkers. Clear boundaries build mutual respect.

- **Foundation of Self-Worth.** Setting boundaries is a way of saying, "This is what I value, and I deserve to have those values respected."

- **Empowerment Tool.** Boundaries give us choices. Instead of reacting constantly to external demands, we actively shape our interactions.

Setting Your Boundaries

Identify your needs. What causes you stress, discomfort, or makes you feel taken advantage of? Start there.

Types of Boundaries:

- Consider Physical (personal space)
- Emotional (off-limit topics)
- Time-Related (work hours)

Be Direct, Yet Kind. "I need 20 minutes of quiet time when I get home," is better than seething in silence.

Start Small. Setting boundaries is a skill; try mastering small ones first.

What To Do If Boundaries Are Crossed

Unfortunately, even with clearly stated boundaries, others may occasionally, or even repeatedly, disregard them. Here are ways to respond:

- **Restate & Clarify.** Calmly remind them of your boundary and why it matters.
- **Apply Consequences.** Link their behavior to outcomes (e.g., "If you can't respect my work hours, I may have to limit project involvement.")
- **Distance Yourself.** If the pattern continues, remove yourself (physically or emotionally) and seek support from loved ones or a therapist.

- **Reassess.** For chronic violators, is the relationship worth the energy drain? Ending contact may be necessary.

Setting healthy boundaries is an incredibly powerful tool for protecting your well-being and maintaining balance in your life. It is crucial to avoid the trap of always pleasing others and feeling guilty about prioritizing your needs. Saying "no" sometimes and enforcing your boundaries are essential for achieving long-term balance and well-being. Remember that boundaries are not about isolation; they are about creating the space for healthier relationships where mutual respect and honesty can thrive.

Remember that boundaries are key in improving all types of connections. Communicating your expectations and limits fosters trust and open communication. Achieving balance in your life depends on setting boundaries and knowing when to say "no" to protect your time and energy and prevent burnout.

Building firm boundaries takes practice. At first, it may feel uncomfortable, but that's normal! Think of boundaries as guidelines for self-respect and healthy relationships rather than rigid walls designed to shut people out. Focus on their positive impact on you and those you care about. They are the stepping stones to a more balanced, respectful, and fulfilling life. Remember that you can take control of your life and set boundaries that protect your well-being and happiness.

Benefits of Prioritizing Self-care and Compassion

Self-care is not a one-size-fits-all concept, and it's not a luxury. It's about finding what works for you and making it a part of your routine. Be bold and experiment! Try different activities until you find what resonates with you. Then commit to doing them every day, no matter what. Remember, taking care of yourself is not optional. It's a must!

Chapter 15

Always remember that small acts can make a significant difference. Never underestimate the power of tiny moments of self-care throughout the day. Take a few deep breaths, enjoy a mindful meal, or take a short walk—all these can create pockets of calm in your day. Similarly, do not let your inner critic control you. Challenge it with a firm, "It's okay. I'm learning." When practiced consistently, these small acts can lead to significant positive changes in your life. So take charge of your life by incorporating all these powerful yet effective actions into your daily routine.

If you find it challenging to put yourself first, starting with the basics can make it easier. Ask yourself if you're getting enough sleep, staying hydrated, and eating food that nourishes your body. Remember that stress and exhaustion can make it even harder to make good choices. Focusing on your fundamental physical needs sets a solid foundation for your overall well-being. If you struggle to find time for self-care, try incorporating it into your daily routine. For instance, you can walk during lunch or practice deep breathing while waiting for your coffee. Remember that self-care is not selfish; it's crucial for your health and happiness.

Consistently practicing self-care can help build resilience and make you more adaptable to managing setbacks without spiraling into overwhelming stress. It can lead to a balanced and fulfilling life where you are better equipped to care for others and handle life's challenges.

Ultimately, a well-cared-for YOU benefits everyone around you. You have more energy for meaningful connections rather than interacting from a place of depletion. When you model setting healthy boundaries by saying "no" sometimes, you inspire others to do the same. And, most importantly, the self-kindness you cultivate makes you a beacon of understanding in a world that can be harsh; that in itself is an incredible contribution.

Practicing Gratitude and Maintaining Positivity Daily

Practicing gratitude and keeping positivity daily is a powerful way to move forward after forgiveness. When we focus on the positive aspects of our lives and express gratitude for the blessings we have, our perspective shifts from one of lack to one of abundance. By consciously acknowledging the good things in our lives, we train our minds to see the silver lining even in challenging situations. This approach promotes a sense of contentment and fulfillment and helps us build resilience in adversity.

Research has shown that individuals who regularly practice gratitude experience higher happiness levels, improved physical health, and stronger relationships with others. It's important to take time each day to reflect on what we're thankful for, no matter how big or small. This practice helps us cultivate a genuine sense of appreciation for life's simple pleasures. This can lead to increased feelings of optimism and hopefulness, which are essential for moving forward after forgiveness.

Focusing on what is going right in our lives rather than dwelling on past hurts or grievances can also shift our energy toward growth and healing. Positivity acts as a protective shield against toxic emotions that may hinder our progress toward forgiveness and self-compassion.

Incorporating practices such as mindfulness meditation, journaling, or affirmations into our daily routine can help us stay grounded in the present moment and cultivate a positive mindset. These practices promote self-awareness and emotional regulation, allowing us to navigate challenges gracefully and poise. By prioritizing positivity in our lives, we create an environment conducive to healing and personal growth.

Chapter 15

Conclusion

As we conclude this exploration of the intricate relationship between forgiveness and the brain, we stand on the threshold of a fundamental shift. The chapters we have traversed have illuminated the multifaceted nature of forgiveness, revealing its paradoxical essence as both a deeply personal experience and a complex neural process. Our journey has uncovered the potential of self-awareness and emotional regulation, empowering us to break free from cycles of anger and pain. Through our exploration of the brain on forgiveness, we have learned that this act of compassion can have a profound impact on our mental and physical well-being.

The power of empathy has appeared as a guiding light, enabling us to connect with the shared humanity of others, even those who have caused us harm. We have recognized the significance of memory and sleep in the forgiveness process, and acknowledged the role of the subconscious mind in healing old wounds and rewriting painful narratives. Moreover, we have embraced the transformative potential of technology, such as virtual reality therapy, which can help individuals confront and process their emotions in a safe and controlled environment.

Looking ahead, we stand on the precipice of exciting new frontiers in forgiveness research. Emerging studies using advanced brain imaging techniques promise to deepen our understanding of the neural mechanisms underlying this complex process. These studies are also exploring innovative approaches, such as neurofeedback, for promoting healing and reconciliation.

As we look on to yet another journey, let us carry the wisdom of this exploration into our daily lives. Let us cultivate forgiveness as a habit of the heart and mind, not just as a fleeting emotion, but as a way of living. Let us embrace the power of forgiveness to mend broken relationships, heal deep wounds, and create a world where compassion and understanding reign supreme. It is not always easy, but it is undeniably transformative. May we embrace it with open hearts and open minds, for in doing so, we not only heal ourselves but also contribute to a more compassionate and harmonious world.

Chapter 15

TRANSFORM LIVES WITH YOUR WORDS

A Few Clicks to Spark Positive Change

"We rise by lifting others."

— Robert G. Ingersoll

With a few clicks, you can set off a chain of inspiration and positivity. Your insights have the incredible power to motivate, uplift, and guide someone on the brink of a transformative journey. This isn't just a possibility—it's the real power of your book review!

I want to bring life-enhancing benefits to everyone; every action I take is a step toward that vision. But to truly realize this vision, I need to connect with everyone.

Your role is not just crucial, it's pivotal. It's a well-known fact that book covers and reviews sway opinions. That's why I'm reaching out to you on behalf of those who might need a nudge to embark on their path to a better life through forgiveness. Your review can be the spark that ignites someone's journey.

I invite you to share your insights by leaving a review for this book.

It won't cost you anything but a minute of your time, yet your words have the potential to transform someone's life. Your review could be the catalyst for someone else's life-changing journey. Your influence is immense, and your review can make a significant difference.

Here's how you can contribute: Click the link or scan the QR code below, post your review, and relish the opportunity to contribute to a happier world.

https://www.amazon.com/review/review-your- purchases/?asin= B0CTNTCK6S

Thank you for choosing to be a part of this transformative movement. Together, we're not just engaging in yoga; we're disseminating joy, health, and balance, one review at a time.

With heartfelt thanks and anticipation for our continued journey,

J. J. Nicolls

Glossary

A

Adrenaline: A hormone and neurotransmitter also known as epinephrine. It is released in response to stress and increases heart rate, muscle strength, blood pressure, and sugar metabolism.

Alzheimer's: A neurodegenerative disease characterized by progressive cognitive deterioration, along with declining activities of daily living and behavioral changes.

Amygdala: A region of the brain involved in experiencing emotions, particularly fear and pleasure.

Anterior Cingulate Cortex (ACC): A part of the brain's limbic system that regulates blood pressure and heart rate, and engages in cognitive functions such as empathy, impulse control, and decision-making.

Atherosclerosis: A disease in which plaque builds up inside the arteries, leading to reduced blood flow that can cause heart attacks or strokes.

Autism Spectrum Disorder (ASD):	A developmental disorder characterized by difficulties with social interaction and communication, and by restricted and repetitive behavior.
Autoimmune:	A condition or disease resulting from the immune system attacking the body's own cells, tissues, or organs.

C

Cortisol:	A steroid hormone released in response to stress and low blood-glucose concentration. It is involved in the body's stress response and helps regulate metabolism.
Cytokines:	Small proteins released by cells that have a specific effect on the interactions and communications between cells, often playing a role in cell signaling.

D

Default Mode Network (DMN):	A network of interacting brain regions known to have activity highly correlated with each other and distinct from other networks in the brain.

E

Epinephrine: Another term for adrenaline, a hormone that triggers the body's fight-or-flight response.

Estrogen: A group of hormones that play an essential role in the growth and development of female sexual characteristics and the reproductive process.

Eye Movement Desensitization and Reprocessing (EMDR): A psychotherapy treatment designed to alleviate the distress associated with traumatic memories.

F

Functional Magnetic Resonance Imaging (fMRI): A functional neuroimaging procedure using MRI technology that measures brain activity by detecting changes associated with blood flow.

H

Hippocampus: A major component of the brain involved in memory formation and spatial navigation.

I

Insula: A region of the brain deep within the cerebral cortex that plays a role in diverse functions usually linked to emotion and the regulation of the body's homeostasis.

L

Lupus: An autoimmune disease where the body's immune system becomes hyperactive and attacks normal, healthy tissue.

M

Myelination: The process of forming a myelin sheath around a nerve to allow nerve impulses to move more quickly.

Myelin: A fatty substance that covers the axons of many neurons; it acts as insulation to increase the speed at which information travels from nerve cell to nerve cell.

N

Neural Plasticity: Also known as neuroplasticity, the ability of neural networks in the brain to change through growth and reorganization.

Glossary

Neurochemical: A chemical that takes part in neural activity, such as a neurotransmitter or neuromodulator.

Neurodegenerative: Relating to or characterized by degeneration of the nervous system, especially the neurons in the brain.

Neurofeedback: A type of biofeedback that uses real-time displays of brain activity to teach self-regulation of brain function.

Neuroimaging: The use of various techniques to either directly or indirectly image the structure, function, or pharmacology of the nervous system.

Neuroplasticity: The ability of the brain to form and reorganize synaptic connections, especially in response to learning or experience or following injury.

Neuroscience: The scientific study of the nervous system.

Neuroscientists: Scientists specialized in the study of the nervous system.

Neurotransmitters: Chemicals that send signals across a synapse from one neuron to another 'target' neuron.

O

Oxytocin: A hormone and neuropeptide that plays a role in social bonding, sexual reproduction, childbirth, and the period after childbirth.

P

Parkinson's: A long-term degenerative disorder of the central nervous system that mainly affects the motor system.

Prefrontal Cortex: The part of the frontal lobes of the brain, which is involved in a variety of complex behaviors, including planning, and greatly contributes to personality development.

Pro-inflammatory: Refers to substances or processes that encourage inflammation in the body.

R

Recognize: The cognitive process of finding something as having been previously seen, heard, known, etc.

Rheumatoid Arthritis:	An autoimmune disorder that primarily affects joints, causing warm, swollen, and painful joints.

S

Schizophrenia:	A mental disorder characterized by abnormal behavior, strange speech, and a decreased ability to understand reality.
Sclerosis:	An abnormal hardening of body tissue.
Serotonin:	A neurotransmitter that has a wide variety of functions in the human body, often referred to as the happy chemical because it contributes to well-being and happiness.

T

Temporal Lobe:	One of the four major lobes of the cerebral cortex in the brain, responsible for processing auditory information and encoding memory.
Testosterone:	The primary male sex hormone and an anabolic steroid, important for the development of male reproductive tissues and promoting secondary sexual characteristics.

References

Bergland C. 2015 Apr 11. Holding a Grudge Produces Cortisol and Diminishes Oxytocin | Psychology Today. wwwpsychologytodaycom. https://www.psychologytoday.com/us/blog/the-athletes-way/201504/holding-grudge-produces-cortisol-and-diminishes-oxytocin.

Blanchfield T. 2022 Jan 31. How to find emotional healing. Verywell Mind. https://www.verywellmind.com/how-to-find-emotional-healing-5214462.

Braithwaite SR, Selby EA, Fincham FD. 2011. Forgiveness and relationship satisfaction: Mediating mechanisms. Journal of Family Psychology. 25(4):551–559. doi:https://doi.org/10.1037/a0024526. [accessed 2019 Nov 20]. https://www.ncbi.nlm.nih.gov/pmc/articles/PMC3156929/.

Degges-White Ph.D. S. 2021 Nov 10. The Many Problems Holding a Grudge Can Cause | Psychology Today. wwwpsychologytodaycom. [accessed 2023 Nov 10]. https://www.psychologytoday.com/us/blog/lifetime-connections/202111/the-many-problems-holding-grudge-can-cause.

Easterly E. 2022 Apr 25. Forgiveness as a Spiritual Practice. Chopra. https://chopra.com/blogs/personal-growth/forgiveness-as-a-spiritual-practice.

Enright R. 2015 Oct 15. Eight Keys to Forgiveness. Greater Good. https://greatergood.berkeley.edu/article/item/eight_keys_to_forgiveness.

Ferguson S. 2016 May 17. How to Practice Forgiveness and Let Go of Resentment. Psych Central. https://psychcentral.com/lib/what-is-forgiveness.

Frothingham S. 2019. How Long Does It Take for a New Behavior to Become Automatic? Healthline. https://www.healthline.com/health/how-long-does-it-take-to-form-a-habit.

Harvard Health Publishing. 2021 Feb 12. The power of forgiveness - Harvard Health. Harvard Health. https://www.health.harvard.edu/mind-and-mood/the-power-of-forgiveness.

Kim JJ, Payne ES, Tracy EL. 2022. Indirect Effects of Forgiveness on Psychological Health Through Anger and Hope: A Parallel Mediation Analysis. Journal of Religion and Health. 61(5):3729–3746. doi:https://doi.org/10.1007/s10943-022-01518-4.

Mayo Clinic Staff. 2017. Forgiveness: Letting go of grudges and bitterness. Mayo Clinic. https://www.mayoclinic.org/healthy-lifestyle/adult-health/in-depth/forgiveness/art-20047692.

McCullen S. 2019 Oct 14. Is a Grudge Keeping You Up at Night? Greater Good. [accessed 2024 May 15]. https://greatergood.berkeley.edu/article/item/is_a_grudge_keeping_you_up_at_night.

MICELI M, CASTELFRANCHI C. 2011. Forgiveness: A Cognitive-Motivational Anatomy. Journal for the Theory of Social Behaviour. 41(3):260–290. doi:https://doi.org/10.1111/j.1468-5914.2011.00465.x.

Moawad, MD H. 2018 Sep 25. The Neurobiology of Forgiveness. Neurology Live. https://www.neurologylive.com/view/neurobiology-forgiveness.

Mróz J. 2022. Forgiveness and Flourishing: The Mediating and Moderating Role of Self-Compassion. International Journal of Environmental Research and Public Health. 20(1):666. doi:https://doi.org/10.3390/ijerph20010666.

References

Neff K. 2011. Self-Compassion : The Proven Power of Being Kind to Yourself. New York: HarperCollins Publishers.

Neff KD, Germer CK. 2013. A Pilot Study and Randomized Controlled Trial of the Mindful Self-Compassion Program. Journal of Clinical Psychology. 69(1):28–44. doi:https://doi.org/10.1002/jclp.21923. https://chrisgermer.com/wp-content/uploads/2017/02/OutcomeStudy_Germer-Neff-MSC-RCT-2013.pdf.

News N. 2023 Oct 27. Curbing Overthinking in Teens Alters Brain Connectivity. Neuroscience News. [accessed 2024 Jun 6]. https://neurosciencenews.com/brain-connectivity-teen-rumination-25111/.

News Staff N. 2017 Apr 10. The Neuroanatomical Basis For Forgiveness Revealed. Neuroscience News. [accessed 2024 May 15]. https://neurosciencenews.com/forgiveness-neurobiology-6373/.

Newsom R, Singh DrA. 2023 Jul. Effects of Sleep Deprivation. https://www.sleepfoundation.org/sleep-deprivation/effects-of-sleep-deprivation.

Nolen-Hoeksema S, Wisco BE, Lyubomirsky S. 2008. Rethinking Rumination. Perspectives on Psychological Science. 3(5):400–424. doi:https://doi.org/10.1111/j.1745-6924.2008.00088.x.

Pattemore C. 2021 Jun 3. 10 Ways to Build and Preserve Better Boundaries. Psych Central. https://psychcentral.com/lib/10-way-to-build-and-preserve-better-boundaries.

Staff BS. 2022 Nov 29. Meditation for Forgiveness | BetterSleep. wwwbettersleepcom. [accessed 2024 May 15]. https://www.bettersleep.com/blog/meditation-for-forgiveness/.

Suskind Ph.D. D. 2020 Dec 13. Rewriting the Narrative: 4 Ways to Reclaim Your Story After Trauma. Psychology Today.

https://www.psychologytoday.com/us/blog/bully-wise/202012/rewriting-the-narrative-4-ways-reclaim-your-story-after-trauma.

Toussaint LL, Worthington EL, Williams DR. 2015. Forgiveness and health : scientific evidence and theories relating forgiveness to better health. Dordrecht: Springer.

van Monsjou E, Struthers CW, Fergus K, Muise A. 2021 Aug 16. Examining the lived experience of holding grudges. Qualitative Psychology. doi:https://doi.org/10.1037/qup0000205.

Webb JR, Hirsch JK, Visser PL, Brewer KG. 2013. Forgiveness and Health: Assessing the Mediating Effect of Health Behavior, Social Support, and Interpersonal Functioning. The Journal of Psychology. 147(5):391–414. doi:https://doi.org/10.1080/00223980.2012.700964.

Witvliet C van O, Ludwig TE, Laan KLV. 2001. Granting Forgiveness or Harboring Grudges: Implications for Emotion, Physiology, and Health. Psychological Science. 12(2):117–123. doi:https://doi.org/10.1111/1467-9280.00320.

Wolf CC. 2024 Feb 27. How the Brain Copes with Grief. Scientific American. https://www.scientificamerican.com/article/how-the-brain-copes-with-grief/.

Woodyatt L, Worthington EL, Wenzel M, Griffin BJ. 2017. Handbook of the Psychology of Self-Forgiveness. Cham: Springer International Publishing.

Wu PhD J. 2020 Feb 11. The Power of Oxytocin. Psychology Today. https://www.psychologytoday.com/us/blog/the-savvy-psychologist/202002/the-power-oxytocin.

Image References

Free Vector | Hand drawn human brain (freepik.com)

https://www.freepik.com/free-vector/person-sleeping-bed-background_4434140.htm

Free Vector | Negative feeling Getty Images(Canva.com)

Free Vector | Flow Chart Outline Icon by ADB Gemilang (Canva.com)

Free Vector | Six Hexagonal Infographic Element by RRGraph (Canva.com)

Free Vector | Organic Lined Girl with an Alaram ClockSix by Joyce Caleze (Canva.com)

Printed in Great Britain
by Amazon